HOT SPOT 5

Student's Book

Colin Granger

Katherine Stannett

MACMILLAN

Contents

LESSON	OBJECTIVES	GRAMMAR	COMMUNICATION
MODULE THREE: Our planet, our world			
9 It will never happen *Pages 32–33*	• **Making predictions about the future**	*will* future review	**Vocabulary:** *common collocations*
10 Earth Day *Pages 34–35*	• **Talking about results and consequences**	First and second conditional review	**Vocabulary:** *phrasal verbs*
11 A world of extremes *Pages 36–37*	• **Giving reasons and explaining results**	*because* and *so* review	**Vocabulary:** *environment* **Pronunciation:** *schwa /ə/ sound*
12 If I had a million dollars ... *Pages 38–39*	• **Skills**		**Reading:** *missing sentences* **Writing:** *a letter* **Listening:** *ordering photographs, choosing correct answers* **Speaking:** *choosing a photograph*
Module review *Pages 40–41*			
Extra special *Pages 42–43*	• **Folk tale:** *Crow brings the daylight* • **Mini project:** *Desert fact file*		
MODULE FOUR: The amazing and the mysterious			
13 Mystery and magic *Pages 44–45*	• **Talking about things which were done in the past** • **Describing a process**	Past and present passive review	**Vocabulary:** *ships and sailing*
14 An amazing experience *Pages 46–47*	• **Describing an experience**	Position of adjectives Order of adjectives	**Vocabulary:** *adjectives*
15 It's unbelievably bad *Pages 48–49*	• **Making complaints and apologizing**	Verbs of sense: *feel, smell, see, hear, taste*	**Pronunciation:** *elision*
16 World's greatest mysteries *Pages 50–51*	• **Skills**		**Listening:** *matching and ordering* **Writing:** *a story* **Reading:** *choosing the correct answer*
Module review *Pages 52–53*			
Extra special *Pages 54–55*	• **Memory skills:** *Remembering new words* • **Mini project:** *A book review*		
Exam spot 2 *Pages 56–57*	**PET Reading Part 2** **PET Speaking Part 2** **PET Writing Part 2** *(short messages)*		

LESSON	OBJECTIVES	GRAMMAR	COMMUNICATION
MODULE FIVE: Time well spent			
17 Young Superchef *Pages 58–59*	• Talking about quantity and amount	Countable and uncountable nouns review	**Vocabulary:** *food*
18 I'm in trouble! *Pages 60–61*	• Talking about permission and obligation	*make/let* + object + infinitive without *to*	**Vocabulary:** *prepositional phrases* **Pronunciation:** /əʊ/ and /ɒ/
19 Sell, sell, sell *Pages 62–63*	• Guessing and speculating about things	Modals of speculation and deduction: *could, may/might, can't* and *must*	**Vocabulary:** *advertising*
20 Out and about in town *Pages 64–65*	• Skills		**Reading:** *matching* **Writing:** *a review* **Listening:** *choosing the correct answer*
Module review	*Pages 66–67*		
Extra special *Pages 68–69*	• Mini play: *Who likes shopping now?* • Mini project: *A film review*		

LESSON	OBJECTIVES	GRAMMAR	COMMUNICATION
MODULE SIX: Communication			
21 First impressions *Pages 70–71*	• Reporting what someone said and asked	Direct speech / Reported speech review	**Vocabulary:** *body language*
22 Life without a ... *Pages 72–73*	• Giving opinions • Agreeing and disagreeing with someone	*think* and *believe*	**Vocabulary:** *mobile phone related objects and actions*
23 Barbecue chat *Pages 74–75*	• Checking information and getting agreement	Tag questions	**Pronunciation:** *intonation*
24 It's all about communicating *Pages 76–77*	• Skills		**Reading:** *true or false* **Listening:** *completing sentences* **Writing:** *a paragraph*
Module review	*Pages 78–79*		
Extra special *Pages 80–81*	• Literature: *Oliver Twist* • Mini project: *Dream interview*		
Exam spot 3 *Pages 82–83*	**PET Reading Part 3** **PET Listening Part 1** **PET Writing Part 3** *(Letter)*		

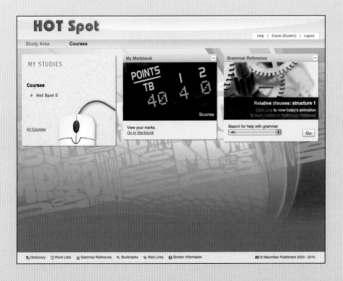

Hot Spot 5 Practice Online provides interactive resources for the syllabus followed in Hot Spot 5.

www.macmillanpracticeonline.com/hotspot5

1 These are my friends

1 Presentation

1.01 Listen and read. What language do Rob's friends speak when they're together?

Blogz   [Join Blogz]   [Take a tour]   Search Blogz 🔍

• • • • • • • • • • • • • • • • **The Rob Blog** • • • • • • • • • • • • • •

Rob's Blog   Profile   Neighbours   Photos   More ▾   Already a member? **Sign in**

Me, My Life, My Friends …

Hello there! I'm Rob. I'm 16 and I'm in Year 11 at Spring Mead School in Birmingham, and these are some of my friends. More than 50% of the students in my class have parents from other countries. Lots of my friends speak different languages at home, but we all speak English at school and when we're with one another.

My parents are from Jamaica but I'm British. We live in a house near the school. Lots of my friends live nearby, so we can hang out together at the weekends and in the holidays. The poster on the wall is of my favourite beach in Jamaica. We visit my grandparents there every year. I love surfing there in the summer. I want to work for an airline so that I can check out all the beaches around the world!

My friend Janiki is half Sri Lankan and half Scottish. She's smart and pretty and the same age as me. Janiki lives in the house next to me, so we spend a lot of time together. Janiki's holding a mobile phone in this picture – it's her favourite possession. She's very fond of texting and sending pictures to her friends. She's really interested in travelling and she dreams of becoming a journalist.

Harry is 15. He lives in a flat near the city centre. Harry is crazy about playing and making music and he wants to be a DJ. He listens to the radio all the time. He's already taken a summer course in audio engineering, so he knows everything about music. He's really sociable, too. He loves going out and meeting new people.

This is Harry's girlfriend, Marija. Marija has lived in England for two years but she's originally from Serbia. Her English is amazing. She lives in a flat above a craft shop in Palmer Street. Marija's the really creative person in our group. She wants to start her own fashion business but at the moment she's concentrating on making jewellery. She's very good at thinking of new ideas. She's quite shy, but she's also very determined. When she gets an idea, she never changes her mind!

Real English

- hang out together
- check out the beaches

2 Comprehension

a Read about Rob and his friends again. Can you find Rob, Janiki, Harry and Marija in the photo?

b Write the correct name.

Who …

1 is interested in fashion?
2 lives next door to Rob?
3 goes to Jamaica every year?
4 is very sociable?
5 arrived in England two years ago?
6 is crazy about music?
7 loves his/her mobile phone?
8 wants to be a DJ?

Grammar spot
Preposition + -ing

When a verb follows a preposition, it is always in the -ing form.

She's very fond **of texting** and **sending** pictures.
Harry is crazy **about playing** and **making** music.

Find these sentences in the text and complete them with the correct preposition and -ing form.

1 She dreams _____ a journalist.
2 She's really interested _____.
3 She's concentrating _____ jewellery.
4 She's very good _____ of new ideas.

3 Grammar practice

Use the prompts to write sentences.

1   She's crazy about playing on her games console.

1   she/be/crazy/play/on her games console
2   Ben and Sam/be/very good/act
3   I/be/concentrating/watch/this programme
4   Greta/have/always dreamt/become/a composer
5   my dad/be/fond/eat/biscuits
6   I/be/interested/work/with animals

4 Vocabulary

a   Find adjectives in the text that mean the same as these words.

1   outgoing   4   attractive
2   clever   5   introverted
3   artistic   6   strong-minded

b   Use the adjectives from the text to complete the sentences.

1   He was very _____ and loved to paint pictures and make up stories.
2   I don't like parties with lots of people because I'm quite _____.
3   She passed all her exams without revising. She's really _____.
4   My uncle Billy is very _____. He loves meeting my friends.
5   Erica is quite a _____ person and she knows exactly what she wants in life.
6   Helen is very _____, with long blond hair and blue eyes.

5 Listening

a   【1.02】 Listen to Rob and Janiki. Who is Jehan?

b   【1.02】 Listen again and complete the description.

Jehan is Janiki's ¹ _____.
He's ² _____ years old and he lives on ³ _____ in ⁴ _____. He's crazy about ⁵ _____ and ⁶ _____. He wants to be a ⁷ _____. His favourite possession is his ⁸ _____.

6 Speaking

Ask and answer in pairs. Write notes about your classmate. Then find out about another classmate.

1   Where are you from?
2   Where are your parents from?
3   Where do you live?
4   What are you good at/interested in?
5   What do you dream of becoming?
6   What's your favourite possession and why?

Useful expressions

Giving personal information

I'm from …	Slovenia/a small village
I live …	in a house/flat/the suburbs
I've lived here	since 2007/for 15 years
I love	making jewellery/drawing
I want to be/ I dream of becoming …	a teacher/a journalist
My favourite possession is my …	mobile phone/jacket/mp3 player

7 Writing

Write about yourself and two classmates. Use your notes from Activity 6.

I'm Jakub. I'm from Tábor in the Czech Republic, but my parents are originally from Prague. We live in a big flat in the west of Tábor. I'm good at science and maths and I dream of becoming a vet one day. My favourite possession is my dog, Nero! He's crazy about eating – food, furniture, clothes … anything he finds!

My friend, Ivana, is also from Tábor. She lives …

8 Check your English

Choose the correct option.

Suzie lives in a house ¹ *in/under* the suburbs. She's crazy ² *about/for* playing basketball and football. She's also good ³ *in/at* swimming, running and cycling. She dreams ⁴ *of being/to be* a triathlete. She does two hours of training every day – she's very ⁵ *creative/determined*. Suzie's brother, Tom, is very interested ⁶ *to study/in studying* psychology. He's at the top of his class in most subjects – he's really ⁷ *smart/pretty*, but he's also ⁸ *shy/sociable*, with lots of friends.

2 One day, one time …

1 Presentation

1.03 Listen and read. Match the times and places with the texts.

1 7.30 pm, Alice Springs, Australia
2 12.00 pm, Malawi, Africa
3 10.00 am, Edinburgh, Scotland
4 2.00 am, Barrow, Alaska

File Edit View History Tools Window Help

PODCAST AROUND THE WORLD

It's ten o'clock in the morning on Friday, 15th May, here in London, England. Let's find out what teenagers around the world are getting up to right now.

a

Hi, I'm Finlay, and I'm **carrying out** a chemistry experiment in the science lab at school with my classmates. We're melting two metals – tin and lead – and mixing them together to make an alloy. Most of our lessons are 45 minutes long, but the chemistry lesson today is a double lesson, so it lasts one and half hours. I like science, but I'm **looking forward to** the weekend! My weekend starts at quarter past three this afternoon – as soon as school finishes. I'm meeting up with my friends Ryan, Jack and Amy straight after school and we're having a band rehearsal. Our band, River Runway, is competing in a 'Battle of the Bands' gig on Saturday night. I'm really excited!

b

Hello. My name's Madison, and I'm 15 years old. Although it's the middle of the night, as you can see, I'm not sleeping! It's very difficult to get to sleep here in the summer months because from 10 May to 2 August the sun doesn't set and we have sunlight 24 hours a day. I usually put aluminum foil on my window to keep my room dark at night time, but I often **stay up** all night long. So, although I feel tired, I'm using my time well … I'm **filling in** a form for my driver's licence because I want to learn how to drive. Where I live, we can start driving lessons when we are 14 years old!

c

Hi there! I'm William and I live in the hot desert part of my country. It's already dark where we live because it's early evening here. In the summer months, I go out bushtuckering with my cousins (like in this photo). That means that we look for food in the desert. But now I'm listening to the radio and I'm also **putting off** doing my homework! At my school we speak two languages – English and our indigenous language, Arrernte. So I think my homework is twice as difficult!

d

My name is Malita and I'm fourteen years old. Now, it's the middle of the day and I'm **looking after** my grandmother's cows. They try to **run away** all the time, so it's a difficult job! I don't go to school because it's too expensive and my parents need me to help on our farm. My morning starts as soon as it gets light. I **get up** at five o'clock and I do the chores – I fetch water, chop wood for the fire and prepare our morning meal. We don't have electricity here, so when it gets dark, at about seven o'clock in the evening, I go to bed.

---

2 Comprehension

Read the texts again and answer the questions.

1 What is Finlay doing?
2 When does his weekend start?
3 Why is Madison not sleeping?
4 Is William looking for food in the desert?
5 Is he doing his homework?
6 What is Malita doing?
7 What time does she get up in the morning?
8 Does she go to school?

Grammar spot
Present tense review

Look at the examples and choose the correct option to complete the rules.

- We use the **present simple** to talk about *repeated actions or habits/the future.*
  I **get** up at five o'clock and I **do** the chores.

- We use the **present continuous** to talk about what *happened in the past/ is happening now.*
  I'm **listening** to the radio.   We're **melting** two metals.

- We also use the **present continuous** to talk about *future predictions/things we have planned or arranged to do in the future.*
  I'm **meeting** up with my friends straight after school and we're **having** a band rehearsal.

Some verbs are not normally used in the continuous form.
  I **like** science.   I **feel** tired.

Grammar page 92

3 Grammar practice

a Complete the text with the correct form of the verb in brackets.

Now it's three o'clock on Saturday, 16 May. What ¹ _____ Finlay _____ (do) today?

What ² _____ (I/do) at the moment? Well, I'm with my friends Ryan, Jack and Amy. Our band, River Runway, ³ _____ (compete) in a Battle of the Bands gig tonight, so we ⁴ _____ (practise) our songs. Ryan and I ⁵ _____ (play) the guitar and Jack ⁶ _____ (sing). Amy usually ⁷ _____ (sing) as well, but she ⁸ _____ (not/feel) very well at the moment, so she ⁹ _____ (take) a break and ¹⁰ _____ (listen) to the rest of us. I ¹¹ _____ (hope) she gets better soon, because she's much better at singing than Jack!

b Look at these plans for the 'Battle of the Bands' gig tonight. Use the information to complete the conversation between Finlay and Amy.

> 19.30 meet at the venue
> 20.00 do the sound check
> 20.30 first band goes on stage
> 21.15 we play!
> 22.30 last band performs
> 23.00 they announce the winners

Amy So, what's happening tonight, what are the plans?

Finlay Well, we *'re meeting* at the venue at half past seven and then we ¹ _____ at eight o'clock.

Amy OK. When ² _____ the first band _____ on stage?

Finlay At half past eight. We ³ _____ at quarter past nine.

Amy And when ⁴ _____ the last band _____?

Finlay At half past ten. And then they ⁵ _____ the winners at eleven o'clock.

c  Listen and check your answers.

4 Listening and speaking

a (1.05) Anna, Natasha and Benedict are in Montreal, Canada. It's one o'clock on Saturday afternoon. Listen and write the correct name.

Who is …?
1 enjoying the weather
2 using a mobile phone
3 doing some exercise
4 staying at home
5 spending money
6 chasing birds

b Imagine you are taking part in the 'Podcast around the world'. Make notes about what you usually do on Saturday afternoon.

> meet friends in town
>
> go to café together

c Now work in small groups. Use your notes and act out a mini podcast.

> *Hello, my name's Sofia, and I'm 15 years old. It's three o'clock in the afternoon in Kiev and I'm meeting my friends in town. We're eating some cake in a café …*

5 Song

(1.06) Find the song *It's a beautiful day* on page 84.

6 Vocabulary

Find the phrasal verbs 1–8 in bold in the text in Activity 1. Then match them with the phrases.

1	fill in	a	my baby sister
2	carry out	b	my best friend's party
3	stay up	c	a job application form
4	get up	d	from home
5	look after	e	very early in the morning
6	look forward to	f	finishing my school project
7	put off	g	a dangerous experiment
8	run away	h	until after midnight

7 Check your English

Write sentences about:

- three things you do every day on holiday
- one thing you're doing at the moment
- one thing you're putting off at the moment
- two things you're doing tomorrow

3 Real history, real lives

1 Presentation

a Look at the picture and answer the questions.

1 Do you know who these children are?
2 Where do you think they are going?
3 When do you think the picture was taken?

b [1.07] Now listen and read and check your answers.

In this week's issue of

Real History, Real Lives

we meet Percy Tuffnell. Percy tells us about life as an evacuee during the Second World War.

When I was five years old, I left my family and my home in East London and moved to a different house with different people. I lived with people I'd never met before.

Why? Well, when I was five, in 1939, the Second World War had just started. The government was worried about bombs falling in the big cities. So they wanted to evacuate the children to the countryside, where they were safer.

6th September 1939, was the day of our evacuation. In the morning, I got up and put on my school uniform as usual. We used to wear the same uniform in the winter and summer – grey shorts, long socks, a shirt, a tie, a coat and a cap. My parents packed a small suitcase for me, with a few clothes in it, and they put a label on my coat pocket with my name on it. I had a small packet of food – just enough for one day – and my gas mask, of course, as well. We used to take our gas masks everywhere!

All the children from my neighbourhood walked to the town hall. When we got to the town hall, we said goodbye to our parents. While I was talking to the other children and we were all getting excited about our journey, my mother and father walked away quickly. At the time, I thought they were angry but now of course, I realise that they were very sad.

Then, when all the children had arrived in the hall, we took the bus to the train station. From there we travelled on a train to Shropshire – about two hundred and fifty kilometres away in the countryside.

As we travelled further and further away from London, some children were crying but most of us were singing songs and we were trying to imagine our new homes. I was looking out of the window at the countryside and the houses and I felt scared but also really excited.

2 Comprehension

Read the text again. Are these sentences true (T) or false (F)?

1 Percy moved to the countryside with his family in 1939.
2 Children were safer in the countryside than in the cities because there were bombs in the cities.
3 Percy wore his summer school uniform on 6 September 1939.
4 Percy didn't always take his gas mask with him.
5 The children went to Shropshire by train.
6 All of the children were happy about their adventure.

Grammar spot
Past tense review

Match the rules with the examples.

1 We use the past simple to talk about actions and situations in the past.
2 We use the past continuous to talk about something that was in progress at a past time.
3 We use the past perfect to talk about something that happened before a point in the past.
4 We use *used to* to talk about past habits or situations that are finished now.

a We **were singing** songs and we **were trying** to imagine our new homes.
b My parents **packed** a suitcase and **put** a label on my coat pocket.
c We **used to** take our gas masks everywhere!
d When I was five, in 1939, the Second World War **had just started**.

Grammar page 93

3 Grammar practice

Choose the correct option.

1 My dad *was waving/had waved* as I got onto the bus.
2 Before I *moved/was moving* to Shropshire, I *didn't spend/had never spent* a night away from home.
3 We *had looked/looked* out of the train window and *had seen/saw* fields, rivers and woods.
4 I *was riding/used to ride* my bike to school every day.
5 We *were moving/had moved* to the countryside before the first bombs fell on London.

4 Pronunciation

a 〔1.08〕 Listen to three past simple verbs.

/t/	/d/	/ɪd/
walked	moved	started

b Now write these verbs under the correct sound.

packed   visited   wanted   lived   arranged   looked

c 〔1.09〕 Listen and check your answers.

5 Vocabulary

Label the picture with these words.

packet
suitcase
evacuee
cap
tie
label

1 ____
2 ____
3 ____
4 ____
5 ____
6 ____

6 Speaking and reading

Work with a classmate. Student A, turn to page 86. Student B, turn to page 88. Ask and answer the questions.

7 Writing

Use your notes from Activity 6 to write another paragraph about Percy. Then turn to page 88 (Student A) or 86 (Student B) and compare your writing with the text there.

8 Listening

a 〔1.10〕 Listen to Percy talking about his life in Shropshire. Which things does he mention?

school   cinema   music
milk cart   food   bombs   pigs
spiders   cats   mice

b 〔1.10〕 Try to answer these questions from memory. Then listen again and check your answers.

1 How did Percy get to school?
2 Did he enjoy school?
3 What did he do in the afternoon?
4 Where was the toilet on the farm?
5 Why didn't he want to use the toilet after dark?

9 Check your English

Underline these tenses in the story below: past simple, past continuous, past perfect and *used to*. Label each tense.

past simple
Before we <u>lived</u> in Africa, my sister and I had never seen an elephant. But when I was six years old, my family moved to a small village in Zambia. The first night we were sleeping in our bedroom when we heard a strange sound. We opened the window and looked into the garden. An elephant was eating the flowers in our garden!

In England we used to see cats, birds and foxes in our garden but we never saw an elephant!

Hot Spot

Talented teenagers

An Amazing New Year's Party

It was 1st January, 2010 and Katie Walter, aged 17, was celebrating New Year's Eve in a very unusual way. She wasn't watching TV or dancing at a party, she was sitting in a frozen tent at the South Pole. Katie was celebrating her amazing achievement of becoming the youngest person to reach the South Pole. 'It was a very good time for a celebration,' she said.

She had arrived at the South Pole the day before, on 31st December, 2009, after a 180-kilometre trek across the ice fields of the Antarctic. The expedition lasted ten days, and the team members travelled on skis for seven hours a day, dragging their 40-kilo sledges uphill in temperatures that dropped to nearly -40 degrees Celsius. But the cold temperatures were not the most difficult part of the expedition. The South Pole is at a very high altitude – 2,800 kilometres above sea level – and all the team members felt sick and tired because of the lack of oxygen in the air.

They started their journey on 21st December, and by Christmas Day they were over halfway there. Despite the difficult conditions, the team was determined to make Christmas Day special. Katie ate two chocolates and heated up a mini Christmas pudding. She even brought some pink tinsel and Christmas cards with her, to decorate the tent on Christmas Day.

Katie was just 15 years old when she decided to join the expedition in 2007, and over the next two years she followed a harsh training regime. She developed her stamina by pulling two 25-kilo car tyres behind her over long distances.

One week after her victorious return to England, Katie wasn't trekking across the Antarctic or pulling tyres up hills, she was enjoying her normal life as a student at Worksop College in Nottinghamshire. She loves music and sports, especially hockey and she's planning to study engineering at university. But although her life is back to normal now, she's sure that she wants to do some more expeditions in the future.

1 Reading

Read about Katie's trip to the South Pole. Choose the best answer, A, B, C or D.

1 Why was Katie's trip to the South Pole special?
  A It happened at New Year.
  B She had a party with some teenagers there.
  C She is the youngest person to trek there.
  D She slept in a frozen tent.

2 What was the most difficult part of the expedition?
  A the altitude
  B the cold temperatures
  C the heavy sledges
  D the long distances

3 When did Katie decide to join the expedition?
  A 15 years ago
  B in 2007
  C in 2009
  D when she was 17

4 What did Katie do when she came home from the expedition?
  A She went to college.
  B She pulled tyres uphill.
  C She trekked across the Antarctic.
  D She studied engineering.

2 Vocabulary

Find words 1–5 in the text. Then match them with the definitions.

1	victorious	**a**	ability to work for a long time without getting tired
2	stamina	**b**	system
3	harsh	**c**	pulling
4	regime	**d**	difficult
5	dragging	**e**	having won or achieved something

Study tip

When you read stories or articles in English, make a note of the different tenses you see. You can make your own scrapbook with English texts cut out from magazines or printed out from online sources. Use different coloured pens to underline the different tenses.

It was 1st January, 2010 and Katie Walter, aged 17, was celebrating New Year's Eve in a very unusual way. She wasn't watching TV or dancing at a party, …

red highlight = past continuous; blue highlight = past simple

"Meet a Reader"

In this week's magazine, one of our readers, Ben Fairbrother, tells us about his unusual hobby.

Hot Spot

Have you got an unusual hobby, or an interesting experience to tell us about? Leave a message on our voicemail. Make sure you tell us:
- your name
- what you are studying
- what you want to be
- what you like doing in your free time

3 Listening

a 〔1.11〕 Listen to Ben talk about his unusual hobby. Which picture shows his hobby?

①

②

b 〔1.11〕 Listen again. Are these sentences true (T) or false (F)?

1 Ben is a scientist.
2 He is studying drama at college.
3 He is a member of an Historical Re-enactment Society.
4 The society visits Saxon people at fairs.
5 He is learning how to make Saxon food.
6 He sometimes acts on TV.

③

4 Speaking

Prepare a short presentation about yourself for Hot Spot Magazine's 'Meet a Reader' feature. Then make your presentation to the class. You can use these ideas or your own:

- what you are studying
- what your hobbies are
- any special skills
- what you want to do when you leave school.

Hi, my name's Ana and I'm a student at St Olaf's school in Athens. I'm studying …

Find someone who …

Work in teams of three or four. Try to find at least one classmate for each sentence below. The first team to complete the chart is the winner.

Find someone who …   Name:
- loves eating Chinese food.   _____
- has an unusual hobby.   _____
- gets up every morning before 6.30.   _____
- owns at least three hats.   _____
- always does their homework on Saturday morning. _____
- is crazy about basketball.   _____

Review

1 I can use preposition + -ing to talk about interests, hopes and ambitions.

Choose the correct option (A, B, C or D) to complete each gap.

I'm very good ¹ _____ making cakes and biscuits and I'm also crazy about ² _____ them! I'm ³ _____ in becoming a chef when I leave college, so I cook all the time. At the moment, I'm concentrating ⁴ _____ baking a perfect chocolate cake for my sister's birthday party. She ⁵ _____ of having a huge party and ⁶ _____ all her friends, but I don't think my mum likes that idea much.

1 A for	B in	C at	D to
2 A eating	B eat	C to eat	D eats
3 A interest	B interests	C interested	D interesting
4 A on	B for	C in	D about
5 A dreaming	B dreams	C does	D dream
6 A invite	B to invite	C inviting	D invites

2 I know six adjectives to describe personality.

Can you remember? Put the letters in order to make personality adjectives to describe Rob's friends.

1 She's (m/r/a/t/s) _____ and (y/t/p/e/t/r) _____.

2 He's (c/l/o/s/i/a/b/e) _____.

3 She's (v/e/t/c/a/i/r/e) _____, (y/h/s) _____ and very (m/n/d/i/d/t/e/e/r/e) _____.

3 I can use the present simple to talk about repeated actions or habits and the present continuous to talk about what is happening now.

Complete the texts with the correct form of the verb in brackets.

Suzie, Saturday, 9.15 am, London

At the weekend I usually ¹ _____ (stay) in bed until ten o'clock and ² _____ (read) a magazine or ³ _____ (listen) to music on my mp3 player. But today I ⁴ _____ (talk) to my friend on my mobile phone and I ⁵ _____ (walk) to the bus station. No, I ⁶ _____ (run) to the bus station. I'm late!!

Simon & Nicky, Saturday, 5.15 pm, Hong Kong

Today I ⁷ _____ (sit) on the beach and my sister, Nicky, ⁸ _____ (swim) in the sea. We ⁹ _____ usually _____ (not/go) swimming on Saturday afternoon – we usually ¹⁰ _____ (watch) a DVD at home or ¹¹ _____ (visit) friends. But the sun ¹² _____ (shine) today, and we ¹³ _____ (like) hot weather, so we ¹⁴ _____ (want) to be outside.

4 I can use the present continuous to talk about definite plans for the future.

Use the prompts to write sentences in the present continuous.

1 Sarah and Joe/visit/their aunt/this afternoon
2 I/not/go/to the cinema with Billy./I/finish/my project/at home/tonight
3 What/do/tomorrow?
4 I/start/my new job
5 My mum and dad/buy/a new car/this weekend

5 I know eight phrasal verbs.

Label the pictures with phrasal verbs.

I'll do it later.

1 f _ l _ in

2 p _ _ off

3 l _ _ k after

4 r _ _ away

5 s _ _ y up

6 g _ _ up

7 l _ _ k f _ _ _ ard to

8 c _ r _ y out

6 I can tell stories about the past with the past simple, past continuous and *used to*.

Complete the text about Percy with the correct words.

wanted	had just started	walked		was talking	were singing	took
got up	used to wear	put on		walked	were crying	had arrived

On 6th September, 1939, the Second World War ¹ _____ and the government ² _____ to evacuate the children in London to a safe place. That morning, Percy ³ _____ and ⁴ _____ his school uniform as usual. He ⁵ _____ the same uniform in the summer and the winter. Then he ⁶ _____ with the other children from his neighbourhood to the town hall.

While Percy ⁷ _____ to the other children in the town hall, his parents ⁸ _____ away quickly. When all the children ⁹ _____ in the hall, they ¹⁰ _____ the bus to the train station. As they travelled to Shropshire, some children ¹¹ _____ but most of them ¹² _____ songs. They were very excited.

7 Now use the language from Module 1 to complete this activity.

Complete the second sentence so that it means the same as the first sentence. Use 1–3 words.

1 In the past I wore skirts, but now I wear jeans.
   I _____ wear skirts, but now I wear jeans.
2 Please complete this form and post it to the address below.
   Please fill _____ this form and post it to the address below.
3 15.30 – meet John at the sports centre.
   I _____ John at the sports centre at half past three.
4 Henry really likes playing football.
   Henry is crazy _____ playing football.
5 I'm very excited about the show tomorrow.
   I'm looking _____ the show tomorrow.

Extra special

Poem

1 Discussion

Discuss these questions in pairs or small groups.

- Do you look like any other members of your family? (do you have the same kind of nose, mouth, ears, eyes, etc)?
- Do you have any old photographs of family members?

2 Reading

a [1.12] Listen and read. Which photo does the poem describe?

b Work in groups. Read the poem again and discuss your answers to these questions.

1 Why did the poet not recognise the picture immediately?
2 How do you know that this is an old photo?
2 Who does the picture look like?
3 Why do you think the poet repeats the words: *you at seventeen, holding a horse and smiling* and *not yet my mother* at the beginning and the end of the poem?

Owen Sheers

Not Yet My Mother
by Owen Sheers

Yesterday I found a photo
of you at seventeen,
holding a horse and smiling,
not yet my mother.

The tight riding hat hid your hair,
and your legs were still the long shins of a boy's.
You held the horse by the halter,
your hand a fist under its huge jaw.

The blown trees were still in the background
and the sky was grained by the old film stock,
but what caught me was your face,
which was mine.

And I thought, just for a second, that you were me.
But then I saw the woman's jacket,
nipped at the waist, the ballooned jodhpurs,
and of course the date, scratched in the corner.

All of which told me again,
that this was you at seventeen, holding a horse
and smiling, not yet my mother,
although I was clearly already your child.

1

2

3

3 Vocabulary

Label the picture with these words.

| jacket | halter | riding hat |
| jodhpurs | jaw | shin |

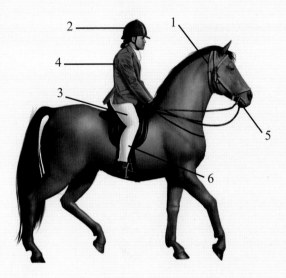

4 Language work

Read the definitions of alliteration and assonance and find one example of each in the poem.

alliteration repeating the same consonant sound in words that are near each other
*I **s**aw **s**ix hundred **s**tars in the **s**ky.*

assonance repeating the same vowel sound in words that are near to each other
*The y**e**llow b**e**droom is v**e**ry m**e**ssy.*

Memory challenge

Learn the poem by heart.

Mini project

1 Read Julie's description of her favourite photograph. Why does she feel happy when she looks at this picture?

This is a photograph of my sister when she was about six years old, with my dad. They're playing on the beach. You can see that it's a beautiful sunny day and my sister looks really happy. I remember going to the beach that day – it was in September and it was the first day of sunshine after weeks of rain. We all rolled up our trousers and paddled in the sea. Afterwards we bought fish and chips and ate them on the beach, looking out at the waves. I feel happy every time I look at this picture because it reminds me of a lovely, peaceful day.
Julie

2 Now write a description of a favourite photo of yourself, your family or friends and say why you like it.

Module 2   Healthy and happy

Lesson objectives
Talking about fitness and health;
Talking about the past

5 Fit and healthy

1 Presentation

a [1.13] Read the questionnaire and think about your answers. Then listen.
Is Alex Cobb happy with Harry's answers?

How fit and healthy are you?

Listen to one of our readers talking to our Health and Fitness Expert, Alex Cobb.

Alex Cobb

Harry

① Are you doing enough exercise?

🅟 Have you done any exercise today?

🅟 When was the last time you did some strenuous exercise, for example, going for a long run or cycling up a hill?

② Are you getting enough sleep?

🅟 Have you slept at least eight hours every night this week?

🅟 How long did you sleep last night?

③ Are you hydrating your body?

🅟 How much water have you drunk today?

🅟 How much water did you drink yesterday?

④ Have you got a balanced diet?

🅟 How many of these kinds of food have you eaten this week?

citrus fruit   other kinds of fruit   meat   salad
green vegetables   other kinds of vegetables
fish   pasta   cheese   rice   bread   cereals

🅟 What did you have for your last meal?

b [1.14] Listen to the questions. Answer them for Harry.

1 Has Harry done any exercise today?

Yes, he has. He walked to school.

2 Comprehension

What is Alex Cobb's advice? Answer the questions.

1 How often should you do exercise?
2 How much sleep should teenagers get every night?
3 How much water should you drink every day?
4 What should you eat?

Grammar spot
Present perfect and past simple review

Look at the examples of the **present perfect** and the **past simple**.
A Have you **done** any exercise today?
B Yes, I **have**. I **walked** to school.
A When was the last time you **did** some strenuous exercise?
B I **played** football on Saturday.

Now complete the sentences with a or b.
1 We use the **present perfect** to …
2 We use the **past simple** to …
 a talk about a definite time in the past (e.g. last week).
 b talk about an indefinite time that is still not finished (e.g. sometime this week).

Grammar page 93

3 Grammar practice

Use the past simple or present perfect of the verbs in brackets to complete the sentences.

1 A _____ you _____ (sleep) well last night?
 B No, I _____.
2 A _____ you _____ (play) any sport this week?
 B Yes, I _____ tennis on Sunday.
3 A _____ you _____ (eaten) any fruit today?
 B Yes, I _____. I _____ an apple for breakfast.
4 A _____ you _____ (do) any exercise today?
 B Yes, I _____. I _____ (cycle) to school.

4 Speaking

a Work with a classmate. Look at the questionnaire in Activity 1 and ask and answer the questions. Give true answers about yourself.

Have you done any exercise today?

Yes, I have. I cycled to school.

b Tell the rest of the class some things you learnt about your classmate.

5 Vocabulary

Match the sports to the pictures.

jogging   hang-gliding   rock climbing
roller skating   ten pin bowling   running
volleyball   weight training   aerobics   hockey

6 Pronunciation

a **1.15** Listen and underline the stressed syllable in the words in Activity 5.

1 jogging

b **1.15** Listen again and practise the words.

7 Speaking

a Prepare to interview your classmates. Write questions with *Have you ever been/played …?* Then ask follow-up questions using the past simple.

b Interview your classmates.

Have you ever been ten pin bowling?
Yes, I have.
Did you like it?
Yes, I did.
Were you any good at it?
No, I wasn't.

Remember!

been and **played** a sport
I've **been** swimming / jogging / ten pin bowling.
I've **played** football / tennis / basketball.

8 Check your English

1.16 Choose the correct option. Then listen and check.

File   Edit   View   History   Tools   Window

Greetings from Fit Camp. We[1] *'ve been/were* here for two days now and we're having a great time We[2] *'ve eaten/ate* lots of healthy food and [3] *have drunk/drank* lots of water. Last night we [4] *have had/had* fish and salad and this morning for breakfast we [5] *have had/had* fruit and cereal. We[6] *'ve played/played* five sports already. Yesterday we [7] *have played/played* tennis and volleyball and this morning we [8] *have been/went* swimming before breakfast …

6 A feeling of freedom

1 Presentation

a Ask your classmates. Write the results on the board.

1 How many of your classmates have been snowboarding?

2 How many classmates would like to go snowboarding?

b [1.17] Listen and read. Answer these questions.

1 Why is Crista so happy?

2 Why is snowboarding her favourite sport?

3 Why is she training so hard at the moment?

Snowboarding

Crista Bonner has only been a snowboarder for three years and has already won three youth snowboarding competitions. We asked her all about it.

You're looking happy, Crista.

I am happy. I've just heard that I'm going to compete in this year's European Open!

That's great. Congratulations!

Thanks!

You've already won three competitions and now you're in the European Open. How long have you been a snowboarder?

I've been a snowboarder since I was 15.

Why do you like snowboarding so much? Why not another sport?

Snowboarding gives me such a buzz. It's so exciting.

What's the best thing about snowboarding?

The feeling of freedom it gives you. You can do anything you like. Other sports have got too many rules.

And what's the worst thing?

Getting hurt.

Yes, snowboarding is very dangerous – what's the worst injury you have ever had?

I'm lucky. I haven't had any really bad injuries yet. I've had a few sprains and lots of cuts and bruises, but I've never broken anything or had a fracture.

So when is the European Open?

Next November. I'm really excited!

And have you already started training for it?

You bet. I've already done four hours training this morning.

What do you do in the summer when there's no snow?

Dream of snowboarding! No, seriously, I've started training in America so I can train all year.

And what's your biggest ambition?

To win a gold medal at the next Winter Olympic Games.

And finally Crista, who's the best snowboarder you have ever seen?

Maelle Ricker. I saw her at the European Open last year. She was amazing!

c [1.17] Listen again. Make sure you understand Crista's answers.

Real English

- Congratulations!
- Gives me such a buzz
- You bet.

2 Comprehension

All these sentences are incorrect. Correct them.

1 Crista is happy because she has won a competition.
2 She likes snowboarding because of the rules.
3 She has had some bad injuries.
4 She is training for the Winter Olympic games.
5 Her biggest ambition is to win the European Open.

3 Vocabulary and speaking

Find the words and phrases in **bold** below in the interview. Then answer the questions about yourself.

1 Yes I do.

1 Do you like to **compete**?
2 Have you ever been in a sports **competition**?
3 What things **give you a buzz**?
4 What things do you do that give you a **feeling of freedom**?
5 What's the worst **injury** you have ever had?
6 How many of these have you had: **a sprain**, **a bruise**, **a cut**, **a fracture**?
7 Are you **training** for anything at the moment?
8 What is your biggest **ambition**?

Grammar spot
Present perfect with *just*, *already*, *yet*, *for*, *since* review

Look at these examples. Then complete the rules below with *just*, *already*, *yet*, *for* and *since*.
I've **just heard** that I'm going to compete in this year's European Open.
I **haven't had** any really bad injuries **yet**.
I've **already done** four hours training this morning.
Crista Bonner **has** only **been** a snowboarder **for** three years.
I've **been** a snowboarder **since** I was 15.

1 We use _____ when something happened sooner than we expected.
2 We use _____ for things which have recently happened.
3 We use _____ for something we expect to happen.
4 We use _____ for points in time, e.g. *yesterday, six o'clock, 2009*.
5 We use _____ with periods of time, e.g. *six years, 20 minutes, a long time*.

Grammar page 94

4 Grammar practice

Make true sentences about yourself.

1 I've just …
2 I haven't … yet.
3 I've already …
4 I've known my best friend for …
5 I haven't had anything to eat since …

Grammar spot
Present perfect with the superlative

What's **the worst** injury you **have** ever **had**?
Who's **the best** snowboarder you **have** ever **seen**?

5 Grammar practice

Use the prompts to write sentences with the superlative and the present perfect. Then ask and answer the questions with a classmate.

What is the most expensive thing you have ever bought?

My mobile phone.

1 What is the/expensive/thing you/ever buy?
2 Who is the/good/singer you/ever hear?
3 What is the/scary/film you/ever see?
4 What is the/bad/food/you/ever eat?
5 Who is the/famous/person you/ever met?

6 Speaking

a Look at the form on page 90 and copy it onto a piece of paper.

b Work with a classmate. Choose to be A or B. Student A turn to page 86, Student B turn to page 88. Then take it in turns to interview each other.

What is your favourite sport?

My favourite sport is tennis.

Write notes of the answers on your forms.

7 Song

1.18 Find the song *Shine* on page 85.

8 Check your English

Complete the sentences with these words.

yet   already   ever   never   just   for   since

1 I've been at this school _____ four years.
2 I've _____ flown on a plane. What's it like?
3 'Can I speak to Ben please.' 'No, sorry he's _____ gone out.'
4 We've lived in this flat _____ 2006.
5 'Have you _____ played hockey?' 'No, I haven't. Have you?'
6 'Can I borrow this book?' 'No, I'm sorry. I haven't finished reading it _____.'
7 It's quite early. Has Alice _____ gone to bed?

7 The rules of the game

1 Vocabulary

Match these six Olympic® sports to the photos below.

> cycle racing   table tennis   basketball
> water polo   judo   4 × 100m relay

2 Presentation

a [1.19] Listen and read the rules for six Olympic sports. What is the name of each sport?

b Read the rules again. What is happening in each picture?

What's the sport?

1 You must wear a crash helmet and your team colours. You mustn't **push** or **stop** your opponents **overtaking**. You win the race by **crossing** the finishing line first. You are allowed to eat and drink during the race and you can **carry** or **wheel** your bike over the finishing line if your bike is damaged.

2 One team must wear blue caps, the other white caps. The goalkeepers must wear red caps. You can **throw** or push the ball through the water with one hand, but only the goalkeeper is allowed to **punch** the ball. You can't **hold** the ball under the water and you mustn't **splash** water in an opponent's face.

3 You **serve** by putting the ball in the palm of your free hand, throwing it up in the air and **hitting** it with your bat. The ball must **touch** the table on both sides of the net each time it is hit. You win points when your opponent can't **return** the ball to your side of the net. You shouldn't wear white clothing.

4 You score points by throwing the ball in your opponent's basket. You can **pass**, throw, **roll** or **dribble** the ball, but you aren't allowed to **carry** or **kick** it. Your team must try and score a goal within 30 seconds of getting the ball.

5 You should **bow** to your opponent at the start of the contest. The sleeves of your jacket and your trousers should be loose. You must only **attack** your opponent's arms and legs. You win points if you can **lift** your opponent above shoulder height or throw your opponent to the ground.

6 Your baton mustn't weigh less than 50 g. You can only **hand over** the baton in the marked take-over areas of the track. You should **stay** in your lane after handing over the baton. You aren't allowed to **start** running more than 10 m before **taking over** the baton.

3 Comprehension

Read the rules again and answer the questions.

1 In which sport are you allowed to eat and drink?
2 What shouldn't you wear when you play table tennis?
3 How many different colours are there for the caps in water polo?
4 What do you hand over in a relay race?
5 Which part of your opponent's body can you touch in judo?
6 In which sport can't you carry the ball?

4 Vocabulary

Act out the bold verbs in the text.

Study tip

Acting out verbs with your hands helps you remember them.

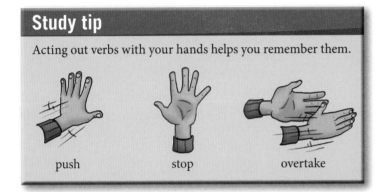

push   stop   overtake

Grammar spot
Must, can, be allowed to, should for obligation, permission and advice

Read the examples.

You **must** wear a crash helmet.
You **mustn't** push your opponents.
You **can/are allowed to** eat and drink during the race.
You **can't/aren't allowed to** hold the ball under the water.
The sleeves of your jacket and your trousers **should** be loose.
You **shouldn't** wear white clothing.

Match the sentence halves to complete the rules.

1 We use **must** a to talk about something that isn't permitted.
2 We use **mustn't** b to give advice and say what is right and good.
3 We use **can** or **are allowed to** c when we give permission to do something.
4 We use **can't** or **aren't allowed to** d when we are obliged not to do something.
5 We use **should** e to give advice and say what is not right and good.
6 We use **shouldn't** f when we are obliged to do something.

Grammar page 95

Grammar spot
Must and *have to*

See Grammar Summary page 95 for the difference between **must/mustn't** do something and **have to/don't have to** do something.

5 Grammar practice

Make sentences about home or school.

1 You must be on time for lessons

1 You must/mustn't …
2 You can/can't …
3 You should/shouldn't …
4 You are allowed to/aren't allowed to …

6 Writing

a Work with a small group of classmates. Choose a sport you all know. Then write the rules of the sport.

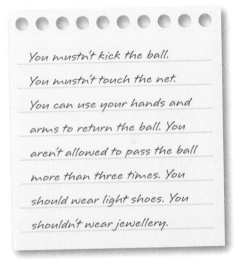

You mustn't kick the ball.
You mustn't touch the net.
You can use your hands and arms to return the ball. You aren't allowed to pass the ball more than three times. You should wear light shoes. You shouldn't wear jewellery.

b Read your rules to the rest of the class. Can they guess the name of the sport you are describing?

7 Check your English

Choose the correct word to complete the text.

The rules of football

Each team [1] *must/mustn't* have eleven players. The two teams [2] *should/shouldn't* wear the same colour shirts. Players [3] *are allowed/are not allowed* to touch the ball with their hands. Only the goalkeeper [4] *can/can't* catch the ball.

Hot Spot

Healthy and happy

Why exercise is cool

What is exercise?

You exercise all the time without even thinking of it. Just by being active, like when you walk up some stairs or run for the bus, all these things are exercise. Playing sports, dancing, doing push-ups and even reaching down to touch your toes – all these things are exercise too.

When you exercise, you're helping build a strong body that will be able to move around and do all the things you need it to do. Try to be active every day and your body will thank you later!

Exercise makes your heart happy

You may know that your heart is a muscle. It works hard, pumping blood every day of your life. You can help this important muscle get stronger by doing aerobic (say: air-o-bik) exercise.

Aerobic means 'with air', so aerobic exercise is a kind of activity that requires oxygen. When you breathe, you take in oxygen, and, if you're doing aerobic exercise, you may notice you're breathing faster than normal. Aerobic activity can get your heart pumping, make you sweaty and quicken your breathing.

So why not do some aerobic exercise right now? Try swimming, basketball, ice or roller hockey, jogging (or walking quickly), skating, football, cross-country skiing, biking or rowing. And don't forget that climbing stairs, cleaning your room and taking your dog for a walk are aerobic activities, too!

Exercise makes you feel good

It feels good to have a strong, flexible body that can do all the activities you enjoy — like running, jumping and playing a sport with your friends. But you may not know that exercising can actually put you in a better mood. When you exercise, your brain releases a chemical called endorphins (say: en-dor-finz), which may make you feel happier. It's just another reason why exercise is cool!

1 Reading

Look at the sentences below about exercise. Read the text and decide if they are correct or incorrect.

1 You are doing exercise when you walk.
2 Being active every day helps your body get stronger.
3 Your heart is the only muscle in your body that doesn't get stronger with exercise.
4 You breathe faster when you do exercise.
5 Swimming is an aerobic exercise.
6 Cleaning your room isn't an aerobic exercise.
7 Exercise makes you feel good.
8 Endorphins are chemicals that put you in a bad mood.

2 Listening

a What do you think?
Why are there so few girl skateboarders?
Discuss this question with your
classmates. Write your ideas on the board.

b [1.20] Listen to an interview with Crista.
Choose the best answer, A, B or C.

1 What does the interviewer ask Crista?
 A Why are there so many girl
  skateboarders?
 B Why don't more girls skateboard?
 C Why don't girls like skateboarding?

2 When did skateboarding become popular?
 A in the 1960s
 B in the 1970s
 C in the 1950s

3 When did snowboarding become popular?
 A later than skateboarding
 B earlier than skateboarding
 C the same time as skateboarding

4 Why does Crista think
snowboarding is more
dangerous than skateboarding?
 A Because of the snow and cold.
 B Because snowboarders travel quicker.
 C Because many snowboarders are girls.

5 Why does Crista think there are so few girl skateboarders?
 A Because a girl's body is less suitable for skateboarding
  than a boy's body.
 B Because girls don't have as much fun as boys.
 C Because girls think skateboarding is a boy's thing.

"Why don't girls skateboard?"

This week's interview is with snowboarding star Crista Bonner.

Sports photos of the week — Hot Spot

3 Speaking

Work with a classmate. Student A turn to page 86. Student B
turn to page 88. Then take it in turns to talk about your picture.

Word pyramid

Complete the word pyramid with these words.

1 the place where you run a race
2 two things you need to play table tennis
3 three kinds of clothing
4 four kinds of injury
5 five kinds of food
6 six names of sport
7 seven things you can do with a ball

track
— —
— — —
— — — —
— — — — —
— — — — — —
— — — — — — —

roll, a bat, punch, bread, cycle racing, throw, water polo, basketball, a cap, citrus fruit, a sprain, salad, carry, judo, cereals, dribble, boots, catch, track, a bruise, a jacket, a net, hockey, rowing, a cut, pass, rice, a fracture

Review

Check you can do these things.

1 I can use the present perfect to talk about an indefinite time and the past simple to talk about a definite time in the past.

Choose the correct words to complete each gap.

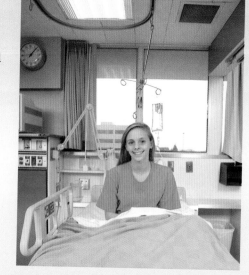

I ¹ _____ here for five days now. I ² _____ it at first, It ³ _____ so strange that I ⁴ _____ the first night, but now I quite like being here. I ⁵ _____ some good friends here. Yesterday I ⁶ _____ cards with two boys. I'm also reading a lot and I ⁷ _____ two books so far. The food's pretty good here too. It's only eleven o'clock so I ⁸ _____ lunch, but this morning we ⁹ _____ a really big breakfast. I'm here because I ¹⁰ _____ my leg five days ago playing football. It ¹¹ _____ a bad break so I have to stay in hospital for another week.

1	have been/was	7	have read/read
2	have hated/hated	8	haven't had/didn't have
3	has been/was	9	have had/had
4	haven't slept/didn't sleep	10	have broken/broke
5	have made/made	11	has been/was
6	have played/played		

2 I know the name of ten sports.

Can you remember? Write the names of these sports. Use the initial letter to help you.

1 v__   2 h__-g__   3 h__   4 w__ t__   5 t_ p_ b_

6 a__   7 j__   8 r__ s__   9 r_ c_   10 r__

3 I can use the present perfect with *just*, *already*, *yet*, *for*, *since*, *ever*, *never*.

Complete the mini dialogues with these words

just   already   yet   for   since   ever   never

1 **A** Have you _____ been rock climbing?
   B No, I've _____ been rock climbing. But I would like to.
2 **A** Has anyone seen Matt?
   B No, I haven't seen him _____ lunchtime.
   C Yes, I've _____ seen him in the gym.
3 **A** How long have you been at this school?
   B I've been here _____ two years. What about you?
4 **A** Can you come out?
   B No, I haven't finished my chores _____.
5 **A** Why don't you want to watch this DVD?
   B Because I've _____ seen it twice.

4 I can ask present perfect questions with the superlative.

a Use the prompts to write four questions with the present perfect and the superlative.

   1 Who/interesting/person/you/ever/meet?
   2 What/bad/film/you/ever/see?
   3 Who/famous/person/you/ever/talk to?
   4 What/expensive/thing/you/ever/buy?

b Write true answers to the questions in Part a.

5 I can use *must, can, should, be allowed to* to talk about obligation, permission and advice.

Choose the correct words to make true sentences.

   1 At my school you _____ use mobile phones during lessons.
     a can   **b** are allowed to   **c** mustn't

   2 In my country we _____ get married when we are 18.
     a must   **b** can't   **c** can

   3 When you are driving you _____ stop when the light is red.
     a mustn't   **b** must   **c** should

   4 At my school we _____ wear anything we like.
     a are allowed to **b** are not allowed to **c** shouldn't

   5 I _____ keep my room tidy at home.
     a shouldn't   **b** am allowed to   **c** should

   6 You _____ sit on the grass at our local park.
     a should   **b** are allowed to   **c** mustn't

   7 You _____ park in the street outside our school.
     a can't   **b** can   **c** must

   8 In my country you _____ have a licence to drive a car.
     a should   **b** can   **c** must

6 I know vocabulary for sports.

Look at the pictures and complete the crossword.

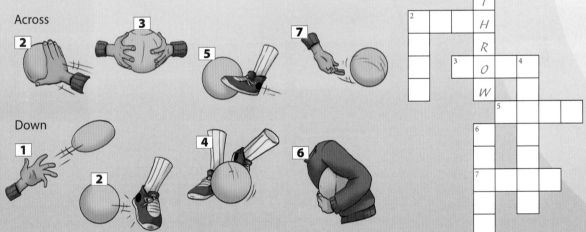

Across

Down

7 Now use the language from Module 2 to complete this activity.

Complete the second sentence so that it means the same as the first sentence.
Use 1 or 2 words.

   1 My health is very good.
     I'm very _____.
   2 I haven't flown in a plane.
     I've _____ flown in a plane.
   3 I can't go out tonight.
     I'm not _____ go out tonight.

   4 I started taking judo classes on 1 January.
     I've been doing judo _____ 1 January.
   5 He left about two minutes ago.
     He has _____ left.

Mini play

a [1.21] Listen and read. What do Toby and Max want to do?

Eva What are you two looking at?

Max We're looking at what this gym offers.

Eva Why? Are you thinking of joining?

Toby We'd love to, but there's no way we could afford it.

Max Yes, it's really expensive.

Lucy Anyway, what do you want to join a gym for?

Toby Because I'm really unfit at the moment.

Max Yes, and so am I. Look at all the things you can do here. You can do weight training. Look at the muscles that guy has got. I'd love to have muscles like him.

Toby Yes, and look at those brilliant running machines. You can really get fit on those.

Max Yes, and look there's a pool. We could go swimming every day if we were members.

Eva But you don't have to go to a gym to get fit.

Lucy Yes, that's right. Max, you get the bus to school every day. You've got a bike. Why don't you cycle?

Eva Yes, and Toby, you get a lift to school every day. Why don't you walk? It's not far from your house.

Max Hey, it's winter. It's far too cold and rainy to cycle to school.

Toby Yes, and none of my friends walk to school. I'd have to walk on my own. I need to join a gym.

Eva But there's a gym at school. Why don't you go there?

Max Because they don't have any cool running machines and weights.

Toby And there isn't a pool.

Eva I tell you what. Come to my house on Saturday.

Toby Why?

Eva Because we've got a gym at home. And you can use it. That's right, isn't it, Lucy?

Lucy Yes, right.

Max What? You've got a gym at home?

Eva Yes. A home gym.

Toby Wow, that's brilliant.

Max Yes, that's amazing. Thanks a lot. We'll come over on Saturday …

b [1.22] Now listen and read the last part of the play. What do Eva and Lucy want Toby and Max to do?

Saturday

Toby	But Eva, where's the gym?
Max	Yes, you said you had a gym.
Eva	Yes, we have and you're looking at it right now.
Toby	What? I don't understand.
Eva	My whole house is a gym. My home gym.
Toby	What do you mean?
Lucy	Look, these buckets are your weights. Feel how heavy they are. So carry them around for a couple of hours while you wash all the floors and that will be really good for your muscles.
Eva	And Max, these stairs make a fantastic running machine. Run up and down them ten times vacuuming the carpet and you'll soon get fit.
Max	Right. I get it. You want us to clean your house?
Eva	That's right. Welcome to my home gym!

Mini project

1 Read Sam's class interviews. Think about how you would answer his questions.

Experiences

What's the scariest thing you've ever done? Bungee jumping.

Why was it so scary? Because I had to jump 200 metres from a bridge. I don't like heights anyway so it was terrifying.

Why did you do it? My friends dared me to do it. And I didn't want them to think I was scared.

Who's the most interesting person you've ever met? My biology teacher at my last school.

Why was he so interesting? He was really crazy but also really interesting. He did really amazing things like once he brought a sheep into the classroom.

What a real sheep? Yes, a real one. And you could ask him about anything. He made biology really interesting.

What's the most exciting film you've ever seen? The Dark Knight.

Why was it so exciting? The story was really good and the acting was great. Sometimes I had to close my eyes because it was so scary.

Do you see a lot of action films? Yes, I do. I love them.

Sam

2 Interview some classmates about their experiences and write a report.

Exam spot 1

PET Reading Part 1

In Part 1 of the Reading Paper you have to read five very short texts and then answer a multiple-choice question about each text.

Tip

Look at each text and think about *where* you might find it. Sometimes the picture will help you (is the text on a phone, or in an e-mail, on a door or on a sign?). When you understand the situation, the meaning is clearer.

1 Look at the five notes and messages below. Match each note with a description.

1   a text message from a sick friend   5

1 a text message from a sick friend
2 a note from a friend about a film
3 a library notice
4 a notice about classrooms at school
5 a label on a bottle of medicine

2 Read the notes and messages and decide which is the best answer (A, B or C).

1

DIRECTIONS FOR USE

Take two tablets with food,
twice a day.

A You should eat twice a day.
B You should take four tablets every day.
C You should take two tablets before every meal.

2

> Please return all books to the front desk
> before the end of term (15ᵗʰ July).
>
> There will be a fine of **£5.00** for any
> overdue books after this date.

A All books are now overdue.
B You should return all books before 15ᵗʰ July.
C You have to pay £5.00 when you take out a library book.

3

> John
>
> Have bought tickets – film starts at 7.30. See you at the cinema at 7.15 – don't be late again!
>
> Sally xx

A John has to buy the tickets when he gets to the cinema.
B John should get to the cinema 15 minutes before the film starts.
C John thinks that Sally is usually late.

4

> There will be a maths examination in the music studio this afternoon. Clarinet, violin and guitar lessons will be in Room 5b. Piano lessons are cancelled for today.

A There are no piano lessons today.
B There are no music lessons today.
C There are no maths lessons today.

5

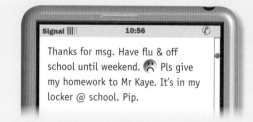

> Signal ‖‖‖   10:56
>
> Thanks for msg. Have flu & off school until weekend. 🙁 Pls give my homework to Mr Kaye. It's in my locker @ school. Pip.

A Pip hasn't done her homework because she is ill.
B Pip is going to school at the weekend to finish her homework.
C Pip has done her homework but she's too ill to go to school.

30

PET Listening Part 3

In Part 3 of the Listening Paper, you listen to someone giving a talk. Then you complete some notes or a form with information from the talk.

Tip

Look at the notes or form carefully before you start listening. This will help you to predict what the talk will be about. Look at each gap and think about what *type* of information (e.g. a date, a number, an adjective, etc.) should fill it.

3 Look at each gap (1–6) in Activity 4 and predict what type of information should fill it.

   a an ordinal number (e.g. 1st, 2nd, 3rd, etc)
   b a preposition (e.g. *in*, *on*, *opposite*, etc)
   c a time
   d a price
   e an adjective
   f a sports facility

4 **1.23** Listen to a sports coach talking about a Fitness Camp. Fill in the missing information.

FITNESS CAMP

Meals
Breakfast: from 6.30 am until (1) _____ am
Lunch: sandwich at café, or picnic lunch – cost (2) _____
Supper: in Meeting Room on the (3) _____ floor

Special guest, Steve Wilson, will talk about (4) _____ exercise and running techniques

Facilities
six (5) _____
open-air swimming pool
gym
running track
Sports shop is (6) _____ the café.

PET Writing Part 3 (Story)

In Part 3 of the Writing Paper, you have two options. You can write an informal letter or a story. For the story, you get either a short title or the first sentence of the story. You should write about 100 words.

Tip

Make sure that your story has a clear beginning, middle and end. Use *sequencing* words like *at first*, *then*, *after that* and *finally* to make your writing clearer and more fluent. Use adjectives and adverbs to make your writing more interesting.

5 Look at this exam task and put the story opposite into the correct order.

- Your English teacher has asked you to write a story.
- Your story must begin with this sentence:
  Lucy woke up suddenly.
- Write about 100 words.

6 Read the story again and underline the adjectives in blue, the adverbs in red and the sequencing words in green.

A *She picked up a torch from the kitchen and stepped out into the cold, silent garden. The light was shining brightly from the shed window and smoke was pouring out of the shed.*

B *At first she couldn't see anything. Then she saw the light again by the old garden shed.*

C *'Help!' shouted Lucy. 'Fire! Fire! Come quickly!'*

D *What was it? Lucy put on her shoes and a jumper and crept quietly downstairs.*

E *There was a strange red light outside her window. She got out of bed and looked into the garden.*

7 Now do the task below.

- Your English teacher has asked you to write a story.
- Your story must begin with this sentence:
  Tom was late for school again.
- Write about 100 words.

Writing Bank

You can find more help with writing a story in the **Writing Bank** on page 104.

9 It will never happen

1 Presentation

[1.24] Listen and read. Match the quotes to the pictures.

Predictions from the past

We all love to make predictions about the future. But sometimes we get our predictions very wrong …

1 A rocket will never be able to leave the Earth's atmosphere. *New York Times, 1936*

2 Man will not fly for 50 years. *Wilbur Wright, American aviator, 1901, two years before his first successful flight*

3 Computers in the future … may weigh no more than 1.5 tons [1360 kg]. *Popular Mechanics Magazine, March 1949*

4 It will be years before a woman … becomes prime minister. I don't see it happening in my time. *Margaret Thatcher, British Prime Minister (1975–1990), 1970*

5 It doesn't matter what he does, he will never amount to anything. *Albert Einstein's teacher to Albert's father, 1895*

6 Television won't last because people will soon get tired of staring at a box every night. *Darryl Zanuck, movie producer, 20th Century Fox, 1946*

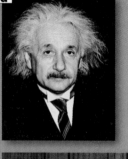

Predictions for today

Those were predictions from the past. But can we get our predictions right today? Here are our top predictions for the next 50 years. What do you think? Do you agree with our predictions?

A We will probably have special glasses with built-in television screens, so that everyone can choose their own programmes. We won't fall out anymore over what to watch in the evenings, but we will lead increasingly isolated lives.

B In the future we will build a greenhouse on Mars and grow food for the people on Earth.

C We will use our watches for all our technological needs. Laptops, netbooks, even phones will seem huge and heavy to the children of the future.

D Cars, buses, trams and trains will disappear from sight. In the future we're likely to have all our roads and tracks underground. Our cities will be calm and peaceful.

E Somewhere at a school today, there is a child who will grow up to become an expert in science and biology and this person will develop a cure for all known diseases.

F In the next 50 years, we are likely to elect a President of the World.

2 Comprehension

Find one quote from *Predictions from the past* and one quote from *Predictions for today* for each category below.

	Predictions from the past	Predictions for today
transport	2	D
space travel	__	__
entertainment	__	__
scientists	__	__
technology	__	__
politics	__	__

Grammar spot
Will future review

Complete the examples with words from the text.

- We use *will* future (*will*/*won't* + infinitive without *to*) for predictions about the future.

  We _____ a greenhouse on Mars.
  Television _____.

- We can also use *is/are likely* + infinitive for predictions about the future.

  We **are likely** _____ a President of the World.
  In the future we're likely _____ all our roads underground.

Notice that we use the word *probably* to show that we are not completely certain.

We _____ **probably** _____ special glasses with built-in television screens.

3 Grammar practice

a Complete the predictions with these words.

likely	will	have	probably	to	won't	won't	'll

Rob   I think there ¹ _____ be traditional books in the future. People ² _____ download novels and information onto their mobile phones and they ³ _____ read everything on their phone screens. We will ⁴ _____ forget how to write with a pen or a pencil because we're ⁵ _____ to use computer keyboards to write everything.

Harry   I don't agree. I'm not sure, but I think we'll probably always ⁶ _____ traditional books. We're likely ⁷ _____ use ebooks more often, but we ⁸ _____ stop using traditional books completely.

b [1.25] Listen and check your answers.

4 Vocabulary

a Find words and phrases highlighted in the predictions that mean the same as these phrases.

1 it's not important   *it doesn't matter*
2 alone, without other people
3 become successful
4 continue for a long period of time
5 think that something is boring
6 argue or disagree

b Write a sentence for each word or phrase.

It doesn't matter if it's raining. I want to go for a walk.

Study tip

Make up your own sentences to show the meanings of new words or phrases. This will help you to remember the meaning.

5 Speaking

a Work in small groups. Discuss your ideas for the future. Try to think of:

- a piece of technology we use today that won't last
- a new form of transport for the future
- a career that doesn't exist now but will in the future

b Choose one of your group's ideas and present it to the rest of the class. Take a class vote. Which idea is the most/least likely to happen?

> *In our group we think that the modern car won't last in the future. Roads will become too busy and …*

6 Writing

Write about your predictions for the future. Use some of the ideas from Activity 5 and your own ideas. Write at least one sentence for each category.

- transport
- future jobs
- technology
- space travel
- entertainment

7 Check your English

Find and correct the mistakes.

1 We won't ~~be~~ use trains or buses in the future.
2 People are likely to forgetting how to ride a bike.
3 In the future, people won't fall off any more about who will do the chores.
4 We will soon get tiring of reality shows on TV.
5 Social networking sites and these kinds of websites won't lasting.
6 There will probably lots of jobs for space architects in the future.

10 Earth Day

1 Presentation

a Work in small groups. Read the questions below and discuss your ideas.

1 What is Earth Day?
2 What kinds of activities do schools do on Earth Day?
3 Does your school do anything special for Earth Day?

b  Listen and read the Eco Club's newsletter. Does it mention any of your ideas?

EcoClub Newsletter
Earth Day – 22nd April

Spring Mead School

Hello Eco Club members!

As you probably know, more than one billion people in 190 countries around the world celebrate Earth Day every year on 22nd April. In Monaco, people take part in a 2.5 km swim in the Mediterranean to raise money for charity. Every person who completes the swim wins an olive tree! In Edmonton, Canada, there's an Earth Day festival with music, dance and art. In Costa Rica, they're celebrating 'Twearth Day' (Twitter / Earth) – and sending messages about the environment through Twitter. And here at Spring Mead School in Birmingham, we're running a special programme of events for the day.

Cloth bags
09.00–12.00

Did you know that we produce 13 billion plastic bags every year in Britain? And did you know that we throw away 70% of these bags after using them just once? It takes 500 years for a plastic bag to decompose! We need to cut down on the number of plastic bags that we use.
If more people used cloth bags or biodegradable bags, we wouldn't need to produce so many plastic bags. On Earth Day we're going to make some cool and very trendy cloth bags at school. If we make more than 100 bags, the local supermarket will give them out to customers in the afternoon and make a donation to our local wildlife trust.

Litter clearing
12.30–14.30

Take a walk in the fields by our school and you will soon come across old cans, bottles, plastic bags and lots of other litter. If we each spent two hours a week picking up litter, the parks and rivers in our town wouldn't be so polluted. So on Earth Day we're asking students to spend two hours helping us to clear up our local park and river. But be prepared – it's a messy job! Unless you want to get very wet, you'll need to bring some wellies, a waterproof jacket and some thick gloves.

Recycling campaign
14.30–16.00

We don't recycle enough! If we recycled all the aluminium cans in the UK, we would have 14 million fewer full dustbins every year! For Earth Day, we want to encourage more people to recycle. Turn up to our campaign workshop on Friday afternoon in the ICT suite, check out our list of facts about recycling and then develop your own presentation on the computer to promote recycling. There's a competition for the best presentation, and if you win, you will get the opportunity to make your presentation at the Spring Meads Community Festival in July.

---

2 Comprehension

Read the newsletter again and answer the questions.

1 What would happen if more people used cloth bags?
2 What will the local supermarket do if the Eco Club makes over 100 cloth bags?
3 What would happen if we each spent two hours a week picking up litter?
4 What do you need to bring to the park if you don't want to get wet on Friday?
5 What would happen if we recycled all the aluminium cans in the UK?
6 What will the designer of the best recycling presentation win?

Real English

• cool
• wellies
• check out

Grammar spot
First and second conditional review

Look at the examples and choose the correct option to complete the rules.

First conditional – **If** you **win**, you **will get** the opportunity to make your presentation at the festival.
Second conditional – **If** we **recycled** all the aluminium cans in the UK, we **would have** 14 million fewer full dustbins every year.

We use the **first conditional** to talk about *unreal present or future situations/possible present or future situations*.
We use the **second conditional** to talk about *unreal present or future situations/possible present or future situations*.

Now answer the questions about the form.
1 Which conditional is *if* + present simple + *will* future?
2 Which conditional is *if* + past simple + *would* + infinitive without *to*?

We use *unless* in conditional sentences to mean *if … not*.
If you **don't wear** wellies, you will get wet feet.
Unless you **wear** wellies, you will get wet feet.

Grammar page 95

3 Grammar practice

a Decide if these sentences are likely (L) or unlikely (U) in the future.

1 If it ___ (rain) tomorrow, I ___ (take) my umbrella.
2 If we ___ (not/leave) now, we ___ (miss) the bus.
3 If a spaceship ___ (land) in my garden, I ___ (be) very surprised.
4 If we ___ (have) more money, we ___ (buy) a bigger house.
5 If I ___ (be) the President, I ___ (ban) sports cars.
6 If you ___ (not/finish) your homework tonight, I ___ (not/take) you to the cinema tomorrow.

b Complete the sentences above using the first or second conditional.

c Look at sentences 2 and 6 again. Rewrite them using *unless*.

4 Vocabulary

a Find these phrasal verbs in the webpage.

> throw away   cut down on   give something out
> come across   pick up   clear up   turn up to   check out

b Use the correct form of a phrasal verb above to complete the sentences.

1 My dentist says that I need to _____ _____ _____ sweets.
2 I _____ _____ an amazing blog yesterday when I was surfing the net.
3 I made these cloth bags at school today. _____ them _____!
4 Yesterday we _____ Eco Club leaflets _____ to all the new students in Year 7.
5 Could you _____ _____ your clothes please, Lucy? They're all over the bedroom floor.
6 Tom _____ _____ the garden after the party.

5 Listening

a [1.27] Janiki is talking on a local radio show. Listen and complete what she says.

If I ¹ ___ our local council, I ² ___ our recycling facilities. We only have three recycling bins in this part of town. That's not enough. And I ³ ___ our green areas. The local park has a real litter problem. I ⁴ ___ to keep our park tidy, and I would fine people a lot of money if ⁵ ___ on the streets or in the park.

… if I were Head Teacher of our school, I ⁶ ___ our school bus system. At the moment only 20% of students come to school by school bus, and 62% come by car. And only 18% walk or cycle! That's not enough! I ⁷ ___ racks to the school car park and I ⁸ ___ cycle training after school to all students.

6 Writing

Work in groups. Think about how you would like to change your school and your town and make notes. Then write an e-mail to a local radio about your ideas.

File   Edit   View   History   Tools   Window

To: Radio Hockley
From: Karel

If I were in charge of our school, I would plant vegetables and fruit in our school yard. I think we should …

7 Check your English

Complete these sentences with your own ideas.

1 If I were President …
2 If I went to Spring Mead School …
3 If my school had an Eco Club …
4 If I cycle to school tomorrow …
5 If you drop litter in the street …

11 A world of extremes

1 Presentation

a Look at the pictures of the three animals. Can you match the animals to their habitats?

1 The Mojave Desert
2 The Amazon Rainforest
3 The Arctic

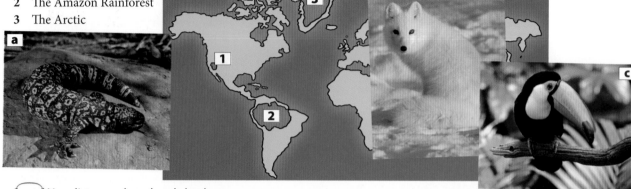

b (1.28) Now listen and read and check your answers.

Animal adaptations

All around the world, in the most extreme conditions, we can find life. From the icy frozen tundra of the Arctic to the hot humid tropical rainforests of the Amazon; from the dry harsh deserts of Africa to the high mountains of the Himalayas, animals have survived because they have adapted to their habitats. In this feature we look at how three animals survive in extreme environments.

The Arctic Fox

In the Arctic the temperature can reach -50°C, so the animals here need protection from the cold. The Arctic fox's fur is perfect for this because it is deep and thick and it also works as camouflage. In the winter, the fur is white, the same colour as the snow, but in the summer it changes to brown as its habitat changes. The Arctic fox finds its prey by listening carefully to sounds under the snow. When it hears a noise, it jumps up and down on the snow to break it and catch its prey.

The Gila Monster

The Gila monster is a large poisonous lizard, which lives in the Mojave and Sonora deserts of the USA. In the summer, the desert sun is extremely hot, so the Gila monster usually hides in underground burrows and only comes out to hunt during the late afternoons. The animals in the desert have to survive on very little water because it rains very rarely. The Gila monster stores fat in its tail and it can use this during times of extreme drought.

The Red-billed Toucan

Tropical rainforests like the Amazon are warm, shady environments with a heavy rainfall – the perfect habitat for many different types of animals. However, there is competition for food, sunlight and space because there are so many animals in the rainforest. The red-billed toucan is well-adapted to survive in this competitive environment because it has strong feet to hold onto the branches of the trees. The rainforest is dark and shady, so the red-billed toucan uses its bright colours to warn other toucans about danger, and to attract a mate.

2 Comprehension

Read the text again. Are these sentences true (T), false (F) or doesn't say (DS)?

1 The Arctic fox's fur changes colour when the weather gets warmer.
2 It catches its prey by jumping up and down on it.
3 It lives under the ground.
4 The Gila monster hunts for its prey in underground burrows.
5 In the winter it hunts during the day.
6 When there is very little to eat in the desert, the Gila monster loses its tail.
7 The red-billed toucan uses its strong feet to catch insects.
8 It is always easy to see the red-billed Toucan in the dark rainforest.

Grammar spot
because and so

We use *because* to introduce the reason for something.
We use *so* to introduce the cause of something.

Complete the sentences with words from the text.
1 In the Himalayas, animals have survived because _____.
2 Animals have to survive on very little water because _____.
3 In the Arctic, the temperature can reach -50°C, so _____.
4 In the summer, the desert sun is extremely hot, so _____.

3 Grammar practice

Use *because* or *so* to complete this information about the Emperor penguin.

Emperor penguins live in the Antarctic. They are very big, tall animals, ¹ _____ they need to eat a large quantity of food. They have to keep warm in the cold weather, ² _____ they crowd together in large groups. The female penguin lays one egg in May and then she goes to the sea ³ _____ she needs to find food. The male penguin has to keep the egg warm, ⁴ _____ he places it on top of his feet for 64 days, until the female penguin returns. He is very careful with the egg, ⁵ _____ it can break easily in the extreme cold. When the female penguin returns, she looks after the egg and the male penguin goes to the sea to look for food.

4 Vocabulary

Work with a classmate. Choose three of these words and find them in the text. Can you guess the meaning?

tundra harsh drought humid
burrow prey shady camouflage

5 Speaking and writing

a Work with a classmate. Follow the instructions below.

Student A Ask your classmate these questions about the polar bear. Then turn to page 86 and use the information to answer your classmate's questions.

Polar bear

How tall is it?
How much does it weigh?
Where does it live?
How does it survive in the cold weather?

Student B Turn to page 89 and use the information to answer your classmate's questions. Then ask your classmate these questions about the camel.

Camel

How tall is it?
How much does it weigh?
Where does it live?
How does it survive when there is no rain?

b Now use the information to write a paragraph about the camel or the polar bear.

6 Pronunciation

a [1.29] Listen to these words from the text. The underlined sound is called the schwa /ə/.

tundr*a* des*er*t summ*er* col*our*

b [1.30] Now listen to these words and underline the schwa sound.

lizard emperor polar danger number

c [1.31] Listen again and repeat the words from Parts a and b.

7 Check your English

Match the sentence halves.

1 Many animals in the desert
2 The Arctic fox's white fur
3 There are lots of leafy trees in the rainforest
4 The Emperor penguin stays in one place for a long time
5 The Gila monster survives in times of drought

a so it is dark and shady there all the time.
b live in burrows under the ground.
c because it stores fat in its tail.
d because it has to look after its egg.
e is an example of camouflage.

Skills

Hot Spot

If I had a million dollars ...

Quincy Watson is a taxi driver and an amateur astronomer. He tells us about how he would spend a million dollars.

'I spend a lot of time driving around the city at night. ¹ _____ You can't always see the stars because of the light pollution in the city, but on a clear night, it's the best view in the world! It's better than anything you could watch on TV or see in an art gallery and it's in our skies at night, every night, completely free of charge!

'If I had a million dollars, I would become a space tourist. I love studying the stars and I've always wanted to see Earth from space. It's possible now to book a flight on a spacecraft with Virgin Galactic. Six  passengers can travel in each spacecraft and more than three hundred people have already booked their flights for the future. I wish I could take a trip with them! It's a two-and-a-half-hour journey into space and the spacecraft will travel at three times the speed of sound – that's over 4,000 km per hour. ² _____ They will be able to look out of the windows of their spacecraft and see the blackness of space around them and Earth beneath them. Awesome! I would love to do that.

'If I bought a ticket, I would have to do three days of training to be fully prepared for the journey. ³ _____ There aren't any age limits for passengers, but anyone who wants to take a flight into space will have to have a medical check. Tickets on a flight to space cost $200,000, so if I had a million dollars, I would buy five tickets and take my family with me! ⁴ _____ So maybe I would just buy four tickets and then I'd spend the rest of the money on a fantastic new telescope. That way I can keep looking at the stars when I'm back on Earth again.'

> We'd like to hear from other readers about how you would spend one million dollars. Write and tell us your ideas. We'll publish the most interesting letter in next week's issue.

1 Reading

a Work with a classmate. Look at the photo of the plane in the article. Do you know what kind of plane this is? Can you guess where it goes?

b Read the article. Four sentences have been removed from it. Choose from the sentences A–E below the one which fits each gap (1–4). There is one extra sentence which you do not need to use.

   A Actually, although my two sons and my wife would love to come along, my daughter hates flying.

   B It will travel up to 110 km above the Earth and the passengers will experience about six minutes of zero gravity, when they will float around the spacecraft.

   C The space flights will depart from Spaceport America, a spaceport in 70 square km of land in New Mexico.

   D I always find it amazing that people can be out on the streets at night time and they never look up at the sky.

   E I'd learn about safety procedures and I'd find out about how to stay comfortable in an atmosphere of very low gravity.

c Read the article again and find a fact for each number.

   1 three — the number of days of training passengers have to do

1	three	4	six
2	4,000	5	six
3	200,000	6	two and a half

2 Writing

Write a letter about how you would spend one million dollars. Begin your letter like this:

Dear Hot Spot Magazine,
If I had a million dollars, I would …

Write no more than 100 words.

"Readers' Photos"

Last week we asked you to send in your best photos on the theme of 'Our Planet'. We received over six hundred amazing pictures, and it was very difficult to choose the best ones. So now we're asking you, the reader, to judge the best from our shortlist. Which of these pictures is the best?

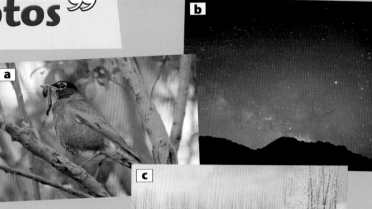

3 Listening

a [1.32] Listen to Orla and Gerry discussing the photos above. Number the photos in the order they mention them.

b [1.32] Listen again and choose the correct answer.

1 Orla likes the first photo because
   a she loves pictures of nature.
   b it's fun.
   c she likes cold weather.

2 Gerry thinks that the first photo is
   a an excellent picture.
   b a terrible picture.
   c fun but not a particularly good picture.

3 Gerry likes the second photo because
   a he likes trees.
   b he likes birds.
   c it's a beautiful picture.

4 Gerry thinks that the third photo is
   a very special.
   b technically poor.
   c good, but he's seen lots of similar photos.

4 Speaking

Work with a classmate. Turn to page 91. Which photo do you like best? Why? Discuss your ideas together.

Now talk with a different classmate. Tell your new partner about the photo you chose and explain your reasons.

I prefer this picture because it shows …

I really like the …

Look at the … in the background.

This picture makes me think about …

What do you think of it?

Twenty guesses

Think of an animal. Your classmates have to guess the animal. They can ask questions, but you can only answer *Yes* or *No*.

Ask about:

- appearance (*Has it got bright colours?*)
- habitat (*Does it live in the rainforest?*)
- diet (*Does it eat meat?*)
- abilities (*Can it run fast?*)

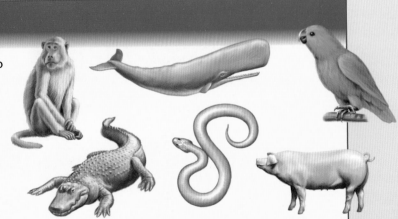

Review

Check you can do these things.

1 I can make predictions about the future.

a Use the prompts to write sentences.

1 In the future/we/live/in special eco-houses
2 There/probably/be/a President of the World
3 We/never/discover/life on other planets
4 Some animals/likely/become/extinct
5 There/not be/any wars/in the future
6 People/live/until they are two hundred years old

b Now answer these questions with your own ideas.

In the future ...
1 ... where will we live?
2 ... who will rule our country/world?
3 ... will we discover life on other planets?
4 ... how long will people live?

I think we will ...

2 I can talk about real and unlikely future conditions.

Match the sentence halves.

1 If I lose my mum's mobile phone,
2 If I moved to Australia,
3 If you wear those shoes,
4 If I pass my exams,
5 If I found a purse in the street,
6 If you ate twenty bananas,
7 If you don't go to bed now,
8 If your best friend forgot your birthday,

a I'd take it to the police.
b my dad will buy me a new bike.
c you'd feel really sick!
d would you be upset?
e you'll be very tired tomorrow morning.
f she'll be really angry.
g I'd miss my friends.
h your feet will get wet.

3 I know eight phrasal verbs.

Choose the correct option (A, B, C, D) to complete each gap.

More than 500 people ¹ _____ up to the opening of 'ReCycle', the new eco centre in Fern Street on Saturday. The centre gave ² _____ free T-shirts to the first 20 customers. One lucky customer, Anna Kelly, said, 'I came ³ _____ some information about the centre when I ⁴ _____ up a leaflet at the leisure centre yesterday, so I decided to come here today to ⁵ _____ it out. I love my free T-shirt – it's cool!'

'We throw ⁶ _____ too many things,' said centre manager, Paul Deacon. 'We need to ⁷ _____ down on the amount of rubbish we produce and we need to recycle more.' ReCycle is organising a litter clearing day next Saturday at Fern Park. They want to clear ⁸ _____ the park and the river.

1	A	arrived	B	turned	C	left	D	did
2	A	out	B	over	C	for	D	about
3	A	over	B	with	C	across	D	up
4	A	picked	B	took	C	checked	D	came
5	A	see	B	know	C	discover	D	check
6	A	down	B	off	C	over	D	away
7	A	make	B	do	C	take	D	cut
8	A	about	B	over	C	up	D	in

4 I can use *because* and *so* to talk about cause and result.

Choose the correct option for each sentence.

1 The red-billed toucan is visible *because/so* it has bright colours.
2 It is very hot in the desert during the day, *because/so* the Gila monster hides underground.
3 The Arctic fox jumps on the snow *because/so* it wants to catch its prey.
4 The Emperor penguin wants to keep the egg warm *because/so* he puts it on top of his feet.
5 The polar bear has thick fur *because/so* it needs protection from the cold weather.

5 I know vocabulary to describe extreme environments and animal adaptation.

Match these words with definitions 1–8.

camouflage   shady   drought   prey   burrow   humid   harsh   tundra

1 a hole or tunnel in the ground
2 a large flat frozen area with no trees
3 away from the sunlight
4 an animal that is caught by another animal and eaten
5 hot and wet
6 colours that hide an animal by making it look like its natural background
7 difficult to live in
8 a period of time when there is no rain

6 Now use the language from Module 3 to complete this activity.

Complete the second sentence so that it means the same as the first sentence. Use 1–3 words.

1 We will probably build cities on other planets in the future.
   We _____ likely to build cities on other planets in the future.
2 I don't want to break my sister's watch because she will be very upset.
   If _____ sister's watch, she will be very upset.
3 I found this strange piece of paper in your bag.
   I _____ across this strange piece of paper in your bag.
4 Only six people came to my birthday party.
   Only six people turned _____ my birthday party.
5 It's very cold, so she's wearing a coat.
   She's wearing a coat _____ it's very cold.

Extra special

Folk tale

1 Discussion

Read the title and look at the pictures. Try to predict the story.
Discuss your ideas in small groups.

Crow brings the daylight

A long time ago, at the beginning of the world, the Inuit people lived in the far north, in total darkness. Their friend, Crow, visited them and talked about his travels to other places, places with daylight. At first, the Inuit people didn't believe him, but Crow's stories about daylight grew in their hearts. Finally, they asked Crow to fly south and bring back a piece of daylight for them.

'I am too tired,' said Crow. 'The journey is long and difficult, and I am old.' But the Inuit people begged and begged until at last Crow agreed.

He set off on his long journey and flew for many days. At last he reached the daylight world. He sat on a tree to rest and saw a woman collecting water from the river. As she started to walk back to her home, Crow turned himself into a piece of dust and hid in her cloak.

Inside the woman's home, Crow saw her small son playing next to a box with a bright warm light inside it. 'This is daylight!' thought Crow. Still disguised as a piece of dust, he floated down and scratched the boy's ear. The boy immediately started to cry and rubbed his ear. The boy's grandfather, the chief of the village, ran into the house and looked at the child.

'What's wrong?' he asked. Crow whispered into the boy's ear, 'You want to play with a ball of daylight.'

'I want to play with a ball of daylight!' said the boy.

So the woman took a small bright ball out of the box, tied a piece of string to it and gave it to her son.

2 Reading

a 🔊 1.33 Listen and read the story and check your ideas.

b Read the story again and answer the questions.

1 Why did Crow not want to travel to the South?
2 How did he get inside the woman's home?
3 Why did the boy cry and rub his ear?
4 Why is there light in the Inuit land for only six months of the year?

The ball of daylight was colourful and beautiful and the boy played happily with it for a while. Then Crow scratched his ear again and the boy cried out loudly.

'Are you ill?' asked the grandfather.

'Why are you crying?' asked the mother.

Crow whispered into the boy's ear again, 'You want to play with the ball of daylight outside.'

'I want to play with the ball of daylight outside!' said the boy.

So the grandfather carried the boy outside. As soon as they were out of the house, Crow floated out of the boy's ear and turned back into a bird again. He took the string out of the boy's hand with his beak and flew away into the sky, pulling the ball of daylight behind him.

His journey back to the far north was long and tiring, but at last he arrived in the land of darkness. As he flew down towards the Inuit people, he dropped the ball of daylight onto the ground. It broke into tiny pieces and the bright, warm daylight filled the skies. The Inuit people laughed and smiled with happiness.

'It is only a small ball of daylight,' warned Crow. 'It will need to rest for half the year. But for six months, you will have daylight.'

The people said: 'Half a year of daylight is enough. Before you brought the daylight, we lived in darkness all the time! Thank you, Crow!' Since that time, the Inuit people have lived for half a year in darkness and half a year in daylight. And they are always kind to Crow, because he brought them the light.

3 Acting

Work in groups of six. Decide which roles you will play and act out the story of *Crow brings the daylight*.

Roles:

two Inuit people	the little boy	Crow
the woman	the chief	

Mini project

1 Read Lucy's Desert Factfile. What do you think? Which of the facts is the most surprising?

Seven amazing facts about deserts

- deserts cover one third of the Earth's surface

- 13% of the world's population live in deserts

- it gets very cold in many deserts at night because there are no clouds to keep in the warmth

- there are 1,200 species of plant in the Sahara Desert

- there was no rain for over 40 years in the Atacama desert in Chile

- the largest desert in the world is the continent of Antarctica

- Europe is the only continent in the world with no desert area

Lucy

2 Now find out about rainforests and write a similar factfile with seven facts.

13 Mystery and magic

1 Presentation

a [2.01] Listen and read about one of the world's greatest mysteries. Use the map and the picture below to help you.

b Read the four conclusions of the inquiry again. Why did the inquiry make these conclusions? Find the answers in the text. Then check your ideas on page 91.

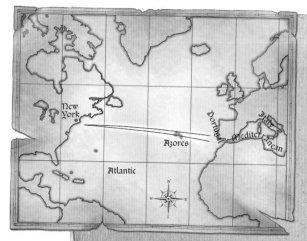

Fact File: The mystery of the Mary Celeste

The Mary Celeste left New York on 5th November 1872 to sail to Italy. The ship was carrying a cargo of valuable industrial alcohol. On board were the captain, Benjamin Spooner Briggs, his wife and two-year old daughter and a crew of seven sailors.

But the Mary Celeste didn't arrive in Italy and four weeks later, on 7th December 1872, the ship was found drifting off the Azores with no one on board. The Mary Celeste was found by another merchant ship, the Dei Gratia. The captain of the Dei Gratia ordered a ship's officer and three sailors to board the Mary Celeste and investigate what had happened. They found that:

- The last entry in the ship's logbook was written on 25th November 1872.
- The Mary Celeste's lifeboat and some of its navigation equipment were missing.
- All of Captain Briggs' family's and the crew's clothes and possessions were still on board.
- The ship's sails were slightly damaged.
- There was some water on the decks of the ship.
- The Mary Celeste was perfectly seaworthy.
- All the ship's valuable cargo was still in the hold.

A government inquiry into the Mary Celeste later concluded that:

- The Mary Celeste was abandoned on 25th November 1872.
- Everyone on board had left the ship in the lifeboat and in a great hurry.
- The weather conditions were bad, but not bad enough to make the ship unseaworthy.
- Pirates had not attacked the ship.

But the mystery remained. Captain Briggs was an experienced captain so why had he put his family and crew's lives in danger? Why had he abandoned a perfectly seaworthy ship in the middle of the Atlantic?

Captain Briggs and his family and crew were never seen again and to this day what happened on the Mary Celeste on 25th November 1872 remains a mystery.

2 Comprehension

Correct the sentences with information from the text.

1 The Mary Celeste was sailing to Italy.

1 The Mary Celeste was sailing to Portugal.
2 There were seven people on board the Mary Celeste.
3 The Mary Celeste was found close to Italy.
4 Some people were found on the ship.
5 The last entry in the logbook was written on 7th November.
6 Nothing was missing from the ship.
7 We know why the Mary Celeste was abandoned.

3 Vocabulary

Work with a classmate. All these words are about ships and the sea. Look at the picture on page 44 and find the words in the text. Then choose five of the words and tell your classmate what they mean.

cargo	on board	crew	sailors
drifting	merchant ship	to board	
logbook	lifeboat	navigation equipment	
sails	decks	seaworthy	hold	pirates

4 Listening and speaking

a [2.02] Look at the pictures showing a magic trick. Then listen to Harry telling Rob how the trick is done. Put the pictures in the correct order.

The coffee cup money trick This is how the trick is done

a b c d e f

b [2.02] Listen again and check your answers. Then work with a classmate. Say how the trick is done. Use the pictures and these phrases to help you.

the bottom of a paper cup/cut off
the two pieces of the cup/put together
tissue paper/push coins/put coffee/pour
the cup/shake the coffee/sink it/absorb
the cup/full of coins

The bottom of a paper cup is cut off.

Grammar spot
Past and present passive review

Active and passive
Are these sentences A (active) or P (passive)?
1 The Mary Celeste **left** New York to sail to Italy.
2 The ship **was found** drifting close off the Azores.
3 The bottom of the cup **is cut off**.
4 The coffee **sinks** through the coins.

Use of the passive
• when it isn't important or we aren't interested in who or what does something.
It's **made of chocolate**.
• when we don't know who or what does something.
My car **was stolen** last night.
• when we don't want to say who or what does something.
I'm afraid the window **was broken**.

We can use *by* + agent with the passive when it is important to say who or what is responsible for something.

The Mary Celeste was found **by another merchant ship**.

Grammar page 96

5 Grammar practice

a Choose the correct form – active or passive.
1 She *makes/is made* her own clothes.
2 Jeans *make/are made* from denim.
3 The 2010 Football World Cup *played/was played* in South Africa.
4 I *played/was played* football yesterday.

b Complete the sentences with the correct form of the verbs in brackets.
1 Our school _____ (build) in 1995.
2 Football _____ (play) all over the world.
3 Two men _____ (arrest) by the police last week.
4 All the windows _____ (clean) every week.

6 Check your English

a Use the prompts to write the story of the Mary Celeste. Use the active or the present or past passive.

The Mary Celeste / New York on 5th November 1872 and / drifting off the Azores / the 7th December 1872. / The last entry in the Mary Celeste's logbook / on 25th November 1872. / A government inquiry / that the ship / on that day.

b Look quickly at the pictures in Activity 4 again. Then close your books and tell a classmate how the trick is done.

First the bottom of the paper cup is cut off …

14 An amazing experience

1 Presentation

a [2.03] Listen and read about the Great Barrier Reef. How many names of fish and animals that live in the sea can you find?

b Write a list of the names of sealife in the text. Then turn to page 90.

A scuba diving experience off the Australian

Great Barrier Reef

Scuba diving off the sun-soaked golden beaches in Queensland, Australia is amazing. Here you can explore the world's largest coral system, the breathtakingly beautiful Great Barrier Reef. The Great Barrier Reef is, in fact, made up of thousands of individual coral reefs and picturesque, tropical islands stretching for over 2,100 kilometres. The Reef is bigger than the Great Wall of China and is so large that it can be seen from outer space. As you dive deep into the crystal clear, warm waters of the Coral Sea you will discover a spectacular coral landscape that is home to an amazing 1,500 species of fish including sea horses and brightly coloured clown fish. Here you can have close encounters with magnificent gigantic humpback whales and swim past dolphins, sea lions and turtles. And for added excitement, take a dive at night and see manta rays scooping up clouds of plankton into their massive open mouths.

The downside

Many people think coral is a plant or a rock, but they are wrong. It is composed of billions of animals called coral polyps. Each coral polyp is about as large as the top of a pin and they form a delicate thin layer on top of the coral. The coral itself is made from dead coral polyp skeletons, which have gradually built up layer by layer over thousands of years. Coral reefs are already threatened by global warming and pollution, but also by scuba divers who kill the coral polyps by stepping on them or even breaking off pieces of coral to take home as a souvenirs.

2 Comprehension

Read the text again and find the answers to these questions. Then discuss them with your classmates.

1 Where is the Great Barrier Reef?
2 How big is it?
3 What is the water like off the Great Barrier Reef?
4 What is coral made from?
5 How big are coral polyps?
6 Why are coral reefs threatened?

3 Vocabulary

Work with a classmate. Find these adjectives in the text. What are they describing? Try and guess the meaning of the adjectives you don't know.

1 sun-soaked golden — the beaches in Queensland

1 sun-soaked golden
2 breathtakingly beautiful
3 picturesque tropical
4 crystal clear warm
5 spectacular coral
6 brightly coloured
7 magnificent gigantic
8 massive open
9 delicate thin

Grammar spot
Adjectives

Position of adjectives
Match the rules with the examples.

1 Adjectives normally go in front of a **noun**.
2 Adjectives go after the **verb to be**.
a Scuba diving in Queensland Australia is **amazing**.
b Here you can explore the **breathtakingly beautiful** Great Barrier Reef.

Order of adjectives 1
Look at the examples and choose the correct option.

When we use more than one adjective together, we normally put 'opinion' adjectives (**picturesque**, **magnificent**) *before/after* 'fact' adjectives (**brightly coloured**, **gigantic**).
   picturesque tropical islands
   magnificent gigantic humpback whales

Order of adjectives 2
When we use more than one 'fact' adjective before a noun, they normally go in this order.
size + age + shape + colour + origin + material + purpose + **noun**
   a **large**, 26-year-old, **grey** elephant
   a **little rope** ladder
   the **metal safety** bar

Grammar page 97

4 Grammar practice

a Underline the adjective then put the words in order to make sentences.

  1 I'm very tired today.

  1 tired/very/today/I'm
  2 red/wearing/I'm/shoes
  3 film/saw/great/a/last night/I
  4 yesterday/sad/you/why/were/?

b Underline the 'fact' adjective and circle the 'opinion' adjective, then make a phrase.

  1 a beautiful blue dress

  1 a/dress/blue/beautiful
  2 flowers/horrible/plastic
  3 scary/a/film/Spanish
  4 maths/difficult/homework
  5 football game/exciting/an/international
  6 friendly/neighbours/new

c Put the adjectives in the right order.

  1 a tiny, round, plastic ball

  1 a _____ ball (round/tiny/plastic)
  2 a _____ car (American/huge/police)
  3 a _____ (young/tall/Russian) boy
  4 a _____ bag (square/large/shopping)

5 Listening and speaking

a [2.04] Look at the photo and listen to Janiki talking about riding an elephant in Thailand. Did she enjoy the experience?

b [2.04] Listen again and find out these things.

  1 Why Janiki recommends the Elephant Conservation Centre.
  2 What a mahout does.
  3 The age of Janiki's elephant.
  4 What you climb to get on top of the elephant.
  5 What the bench on top of the elephant is made of.
  6 What you hold on to when the elephant starts to move.
  7 Why riding an elephant is like riding a roller coaster.
  8 What you can do at the end of the ride.

c Now tell a classmate what you found out.

> *The people are kind to their elephants and look after them well.*

Study tip

Linking an adjective with a noun can help you remember its meaning. Write a list of the new adjectives you learn like this.

Adjectives
scary film
spectacular landscape
sun-soaked beach

6 Check your English

Work with a small group of classmates. Write as many adjective + noun phrases as you can in three minutes using the adjectives below.

> *crystal clear water*

> *warm weather*

crystal clear   warm   amazing   spectacular brightly coloured   magnificent   delicate   picturesque tropical   thin   brilliant   large   little   rope   narrow wooden   metal   scary   gigantic   fascinating gigantic   massive   open   sun-soaked golden   breathtakingly beautiful

15 It's unbelievably bad

1 Presentation

a (2.05) Kirsty and her friends are staying in a student hostel on the Yorkshire Moors in England. Look at Picture 1. Why do you think they are so unhappy? Listen and find out.

Real English

- It's incredibly …
- It's unbelievably …
- Come on.
- It's far too …
- Excuse me.

b (2.05) Listen again and then read the dialogue with your classmates.

c Can you guess how the story ends? Turn to page 91 and find out the answer.

2 Comprehension

Work with a classmate. Answer the questions.

1 What is wrong with the three beds?
2 What else is wrong with the room?
3 Why don't the girls want to open the wardrobe?
4 What is wrong with the three meals?
5 What do they complain about?
6 What does the waiter apologise about?

Grammar spot
Verbs of sense: *feel, smell, see, hear, taste*

It **feels** like concrete.
And the room **smells** horrible.
And have you **seen** those cobwebs?
And can you **hear** that?
It **tastes** disgusting.

Compare:
It **tastes** horrible.   verb + adjective
It doesn't **taste like** chicken.   verb + *like* + noun

3 Grammar practice

Complete the sentences with the correct form of these verbs.

> smell   feel   hear   taste   see

1 This food _____ sweet.
2 Your clothes _____ smoky. Have you been near a fire?
3 Look. You can _____ the whole city from here.
4 Can you _____ that music?
5 I _____ very happy.

4 Pronunciation

a [2.06] Listen to the sentences. You will hear each sentence twice. How many words are in each sentence? Contractions count as two words.

1   6 / 9 / 10
2   6 / 7 / 5
3   9 / 6 / 7
4   10 / 7 / 8

b [2.06] Listen again and practise saying the sentences.

5 Listening

a [2.07] Look at the cartoon and listen. Find the person who is making the complaint.

Can I help you?

b [2.07] Listen again. Then put the dialogue into the correct order.

2	Yes, please. I bought this parrot yesterday and there's something wrong with it.
	It doesn't talk.
	Oh, I'm sorry about that. What's wrong with it?
	I'd like a refund, please.
	Oh, I do apologise about that. Usually our parrots are very good talkers. Have you got the receipt?
	Thank you. And would you like a refund or would you like to exchange it for a different parrot?
	Yes, I have, but it doesn't say anything.
1	Can I help you?
	Yes, here you are.
	Oh, I see. Have you tried to speak to it?

c Now practise the dialogue with a classmate.

Can I help you?

Yes, please. I bought this parrot yesterday and there's something wrong with it.

6 Speaking

a Work with a classmate. Decide who is A and who is B. Then turn to your page at the back of the book and prepare your complaint. Student A, turn to page 87. Student B, turn to page 89.

Write notes to help you prepare the conversation. Use the useful expressions to help you.

Useful expressions

Making complaints	**Apologising**
My shoes are too tight.	I apologise about …
My mobile phone isn't working.	We're so sorry …
My alarm clock doesn't wake me up.	
This chocolate isn't sweet enough.	

b Act out a conversation with your classmate. Take it in turns to play the customer and the shop assistant.

Can I help you?

Yes, please. I bought this …

7 Check your English

Write a conversation between the sales assistant and the customer making the complaint about the alarm clock. Here are some ideas to help you.

> it doesn't wake me up   it keeps me awake
> it doesn't tell the right time

Hot Spot

World's greatest mysteries

The waterspout theory

There are many theories that try to explain the mystery of the Mary Celeste. These theories range from pirates or sea monsters attacking the ship to a UFO landing on its deck and taking away everyone on board. Of all the theories perhaps the most convincing is the waterspout theory.

 **a**

 **b**

 **c**

 **d**

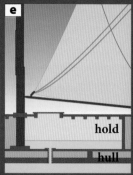 **e**

hold

hull

1 Listening

a [2.08] Read the text and look at the pictures. Then listen and match what you hear to a picture.

b [2.09] Listen again – this time in the correct order. Then complete the sentences with these words and phrases.

> crew   low pressure   a little   sink   daughter   rowed
> lifeboat   full   hull   bad news   abandon   pushed   higher
> measuring rod   showed   hold   waterspout   water

1   The Mary Celeste was hit by a huge ___.
2   Captain Briggs sent a sailor into the ___ to check the ship wasn't taking in ___.
3   The sailor used a ___ to check how much water was in the ___.
4   The rod ___ that the hull was ___ of water.
5   The sailor told Captain Briggs the ___.
6   Captain Briggs immediately told his ___ to ___ ship.
7   Captain Briggs, his wife and ___, and crew got into the ___and ___ away.
8   But the Mary Celeste didn't ___ and there was only ___ water in the hull.
9   ___ inside the waterspout had ___ the water up the measuring rod which made it look ___ than it was.

2 Writing

a Imagine you are one of the sailors from the Dei Gratia who boarded the Mary Celeste. Continue the story using the picture on page 44 and words from the box to help you.

> logbook   lifeboat   sails   hold
> navigation equipment   on board
> pirates   cargo   industrial alcohol
> Azores   sail   find   drift   board
> miss   take   abandon   damage
> valuable   seaworthy   deck

b Read your stories to your classmates.

> *On 5th December, 1872 our merchant ship the Dei Gratia was sailing near the Azores when ...*

Nazca Lines
One of our readers writes to us about one of the world's greatest mysteries

I saw a TV programme about the Nazca Lines in Peru and it was amazing. It was fascinating to discover that there are more than 15,000 huge designs of human figures and animals such as hummingbirds, spiders, monkeys and fish. They were made in the desert by an ancient people called the Nazca around 2,000 years ago. But the big mystery is that we don't know why the Nazca people made the lines. The designs are so large that they can only be seen from the air. So why did they do something that they couldn't see themselves? The programme talked about some theories about why the lines were made. Some people say they were racetracks, or used for water irrigation or even as landing strips for UFOs, but I think the best theory is that the Nazca people made the lines as a present for their gods because they can only be seen from the sky. Why do you think the Nazca people made the lines?

PERU
BRAZIL
Lima
Nazca Lines

3 Reading

Read the text above. For each question below, choose the correct answer A, B, C or D.

1 What does Tony say is the big mystery about the Nazca Lines?
   A We don't know how they were made.
   B We don't know who made them.
   C We don't know why they were made.
   D We don't know when they were made.

2 What things did Tony find most interesting in the TV programme?
   A The designs were of animals.
   B There are over 15,000 designs.
   C Some of the designs can only be seen from the air.
   D They were made around 2,000 years ago.

3 What theory about the Nazca Lines does Tony like the best?
   A The Nazca Lines were a present for the gods.
   B They were racetracks.
   C They were for water irrigation.
   D The lines were UFO landing strips.

Mystery phone call

a Look at the picture and read.

Every night at about twelve o'clock William comes home from work and gets ready for bed. He then picks up the phone and dials a number and listens. Someone answers the phone and says, 'Sorry.' William then says, 'That's all right. Goodnight.' He puts down the phone, goes to bed and goes to sleep. This happens every night.

b Find out why William does this every night. Ask your teacher direct questions to find out.

Does William need to speak to someone before he goes to sleep?

Does he phone the same number every night?

c Look at the answer on page 90.

Review

Check you can do these things.

1 I can talk about active and passive forms of verbs in the present and past.

a Use the prompts to rewrite the text. Use the past simple and the past simple passive.

A valuable painting worth £500,000 /steal / from the Lyle Gallery at the weekend. The window of the gallery / broken / when robbers / drive / a lorry into the front of the building. The robbery was / see / by two eye-witnesses. The eyewitnesses / tell / the police that three men / get / out of the lorry and ran into the gallery. Five minutes later the robbers / see / running out of the gallery with the painting. They then / get / into the lorry and / drive / away. The lorry / find / later in a field outside the city. Two men / arrest / by the police in the early hours of the morning.

A valuable painting worth £500,000 was stolen from the Lyle Gallery at the weekend.

b Complete the text with the present simple or the present simple passive form of the verbs in brackets.

My name is Ejaliah and I ¹ _____ (work) in a jean factory just outside Tunis in North Africa. I ² _____ (make) over one hundred pairs of blue jeans every day. Blue jeans ³ _____ (make) out of blue denim, and blue denim ⁴ _____ (make) out of cotton. Farmers in Benin in West Africa ⁵ _____ (grow) the cotton and then lorries and ships ⁶ _____ (take) the cotton to Milan where it ⁷ _____ (make) into denim material. Then, the blue denim ⁸ _____ (take) back to Africa to this jeans factory. When we ⁹ _____ (finish) the blue jeans, they ¹⁰ _____ (take) to shops in Europe where they ¹¹ _____ (sell).

2 I know vocabulary about ships.

Match these words with the definitions below.

hold   cargo   lifeboat   sails   merchant ship   decks   board   crew

1 to get onto a ship
2 goods that are transported on a ship
3 the place where the goods are kept on a ship
4 the group of people who work on a boat or ship
5 the floors on a ship
6 a small boat that is carried on a ship for emergencies
7 a ship that carries goods
8 large pieces of strong cloth fixed to a tall post on a boat or ship

3 I can use adjectives in the correct order.

Write the adjectives under the correct heading.

> square   amazing   new   spectacular   brightly coloured   picturesque
> tropical   thin   brilliant   little   French   narrow   wooden   scary   old
> gigantic   fascinating   rope   massive   tall   American   golden   large
> shopping   metal   breathtakingly beautiful   plastic   round   magnificent

Opinion	Size	Age	Shape	Colour	Origin	Material	Purpose

4 I can use two or more adjectives in their usual order.

Put the words in brackets in their usual order

1   I bought a (brown/shopping/large) bag.
2   My best friend has made some (plastic/brightly coloured/amazing) jewellery.
3   Last summer we went to a (Italian/golden/sun-soaked) beach.
4   The model was wearing a (plastic/black/long) raincoat.
5   Last night I saw a very (American/scary/horror) film.
6   Have you seen my (round/little/plastic) ball?

5 I can make complaints and use verbs of sense.

Can you remember the complaints Kirsty and her friends made about their room and food in the hostel? Look at the picture and complete the sentences. Use a verb of sense where possible.

1   My bed …
2   My mattress …
3   The radiator …
4   The window …
5   My sausages …
6   My soup …
7   My chicken …
8   Our dinner …

6 Now use the language from Module 4 to complete this activity.

Complete the second sentence so that it means the same as the first sentence. Use 1–3 words.

1   They were repairing the car yesterday.
    The car _____ yesterday.
2   This door is locked every evening.
    I _____ this door every evening.
3   I can't eat this horrible food.
    This food is _____.

4   I can't believe how bad my food is.
    This food is _____ bad.
5   I'm sorry you don't like the food.
    I _____ about the food.

Extra special

Memory skills

We need to process new words in our minds in order to remember them.
Here are some ideas you could use.

1 Visual imagery

Think of an image to help you remember a new word.

Match these words to a picture.

freedom   ambition   environment   charity   campaign

2 Categories

Collect new words together in category groups.

Write five words in each category.

sport	size	ship	cook	injuries

gigantic **crew** points **serve** opponent
burn sprain cut huge **thick** contest minute
cargo deck **bruise** player sail **fold** fry
tiny chop up fracture hull mix **goal**

3 Process categories

Process the words in a category to help you remember the meaning of each word.

Match each verb with one of the phrases in the box.

Ways of moving a ball

1 punch
2 kick
3 serve
4 pass
5 dribble
6 roll
7 throw

to another player
at the beginning of a game
with short kicks or bounces
with your foot
with your fist
along the ground
with the hand or hands

4 Opposites

Put new words together with a word with an opposite meaning.

Match these words with a word with an 'opposite' meaning.

1 dry
2 serious
3 cheap
4 weak
5 quiet
6 dangerous
7 same
8 peaceful
9 shady
10 light
11 far
12 wide

funny strong **safe** noisy dark narrow
close sunny different loud valuable **wet**

5 Differences

Think of the difference between words with a similar meaning.

What is the difference between these words?

1 *bright* and *light*
2 *true* and *correct*
3 *cold* and *freezing*
4 *wet* and *humid*
5 *look* and *stare*
6 *borrow* and *lend*

6 Pictures and initial letters

Draw simple pictures of new words and write the initial letters under them. Then use the drawings to test yourself.

Can you guess what these words are from the pictures and initial letters? Clue – they are all phrasal verbs.

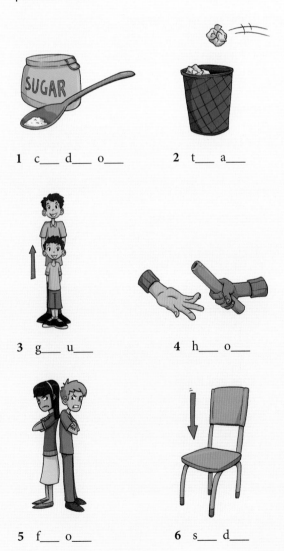

1 c__ d__ o__   2 t__ a__

3 g__ u__   4 h__ o__

5 f__ o__   6 s__ d__

Mini project

1 Read Helen's review of a book. Do you think you would you like to read it?

Book Review: Lord of the Flies

'Lord of the Flies' by William Golding is one of the best books I have ever read. It's about a group of English schoolboys whose plane crashes in the sea close to an island in the Pacific. All the adults on the plane are killed in the crash and so the boys have to look after themselves on the island. The boys are all different ages but three older boys try to organise things. They form a kind of parliament to make laws so they will live peacefully together. This works for a short time, but then they divide into two groups and start to fight each other and two boys die.

At the end of the book, some of the boys start a huge fire and this nearly destroys everything on the island, but sailors on a ship see the smoke from the fire and rescue the boys. It's a really exciting and important story and I recommend you read it.
Helen

Comments

Thank you for this review. I would like to read 'Lord of the Flies'. Tom

I like the review, but I don't think it is my kind of book. Denise

2 Write a review of a book, film or TV programme. Then give your review to your classmates to read and write comments.

Exam spot 2

PET Reading Part 2

In Part 2 of the Reading Paper, you have to read five descriptions of people and eight short texts. The texts all describe things or services of one particular type (for example, eight different holidays or eight different films). You then match each person with the most appropriate thing.

1 The people below are all planning a day trip in Cornwall. Read the description of each person and decide who …

1 is interested in history _____ and _____
2 probably wants to see some animals _____
3 is interested in nature _____ and _____
4 wants to learn a new skill _____

2 Now read about the people again and decide which day trip (A–H) would be best for each person.

Dan is fascinated by early history and culture and he wants to visit museums and find out about interesting buildings on his holiday.

Sandra loves being outside and is interested in wildlife and the natural world. She would like to be near water – the sea or a river.

Rita wants to find out about how rich people and royalty lived in the past. She'd like to visit several different places.

Tim is very interested in the environment. He'd like to find out about different habitats and look at plants and flowers.

Mehmet wants to spend some time outside and some time inside. He'd like to see some of the countryside in Cornwall but he also wants to learn something new.

The Cornwall Experience

A Wildlife Watch

You will spend a day on our amazing wildlife-watching boat, sailing around the coast of Cornwall. Look out for dolphins and minke whales and bring some binoculars for bird-spotting, too. There will also be a chance for you to do some scuba diving.

B Ancient History of Cornwall

We start at the 13th Century Restormel Castle, visit the Royal Cornwall Museum in Truro and then we'll go even further back in history as we look at some amazing Neolithic monuments which are over 4,000 years old.

C Art Smart

Discover your creative skills on this one-day course. We'll admire some paintings at Tate St Ives gallery and then walk from there to Porthmeor beach. During the walk, we'll stop to sketch some of the beautiful fields and the beaches of Cornwall.

D Watersports Adventure

If you love action sports, you'll have a great time on this trip. We spend the whole day at Loe Beach Watersports centre where you can choose from a range of activities, including kayaking, windsurfing, raft-building or sailing.

E Streetdance

Learn how to streetdance at our modern dance studios in the centre of Truro. Our experts will teach you some cool dance moves to the latest Hip Hop and RnB music.

F Castles and Kings

We explore some of the famous castles of Cornwall, from Tintagel Castle in the east to St Michael's Mount in the west and we find out about the legend of King Arthur.

G Eden Project

Spend the day at the Eden Project and learn all about nature and plants. There are amazing gardens here, huge greenhouses and even a rainforest! Admire the eco-friendly architecture and enjoy the organic food at Joe's café.

H Newquay Zoo

Cornwall's biggest zoo has over 130 different animals, including lions, snakes, monkeys and tortoises. You can learn about endangered species and join our zoo keepers to find out about their typical day.

PET Speaking Part 2

In Part 2 of the Speaking Paper, you have a discussion with another student and try to make a decision together. You will have a picture to help you.

Tip

Remember that this is a discussion, not a monologue. Listen to what your partner says and respond to it. Use the language of opinion and negotiating to make a joint decision.

3 **2.10** Read the exam task below and listen to two students discussing the task. Who says these phrases, Carla (C) or Bruno (B)?

1 I'm not crazy about   4 I'd prefer to
2 I don't mind   5 What do you want to do
3 I love that idea   6 Why don't we

You and your friend want to go out this afternoon. Talk together about what you can do.

4 Now work in pairs and discuss the task in Activity 3 together.

PET Writing Part 2 (short messages)

In Part 2 of the Writing Paper, you read a prompt and then have to write a short message of 35–45 words.

Tip

The prompt will always ask you to write about three points. It's important that you mention all three points in your message but still remember to keep to the word count.

5 Look at the task and a student's answer below. The student has made one basic error. What is it?

Your friend has invited you to a party but unfortunately you can't go. Write to your friend. In your note you should

- apologise because you can't go
- say why you can't go
- make a suggestion about another time you can meet.

Write 35–45 words.

Hi James
I'm really sorry I can't come to your party on Saturday. I'm free next weekend, though, so perhaps we can meet up and have a coffee then. Hope you have a great time at your party.
Marta

6 Now do the task below.

You visited your friend for lunch yesterday and now you can't find your mobile phone. Write to your friend. In your note you should

- thank your friend for lunch
- say what part of the meal you liked best
- ask your friend to look for your phone.

Write 35–45 words.

Writing Bank

You can find more help with writing short messages in the **Writing Bank** on page 105.

17 Young Superchef

1 Presentation

a Look at the poster. Choose the best description for *Young Superchef*.

1 Four contestants prepare a three-course meal (price: 12 euros per person) for a restaurant competition
2 A celebrity banquet
3 Young contestants make a cheap three-course meal for a cooking competition

b [2.11] Listen and read. Find the answers to these questions.

1 Why didn't James cook during his first term at university?
2 Who taught James to cook?
3 Why do a lot of people visit James at dinner time?

> LOVE COOKING?
> UNDER 21?
> MAYBE YOU COULD BECOME THIS YEAR'S
> **YOUNG SUPERCHEF**.
>
> The challenge: cook a three-course meal with a budget of just 12 euros for our panel of four judges.
> The winner will prepare and serve their menu at a celebrity banquet in London's Waldorf Hotel.

A STUDENT'S GUIDE TO COOKING

After a thrilling final last night, the winner of this year's Young Superchef competition has been announced. James Penry, a 19-year-old engineering student, has beaten 120 other contestants to win the title of Young Superchef. Here James tells us about how he first got into cooking.

'My first term at university was fantastic! I met lots of interesting people, I spent a lot of time going to parties and playing football for the university team and I even did a little work, too! But I was so busy with going to lectures, parties and sports practice that I didn't bother to cook. I had a couple of snack bars for breakfast, a few slices of bread and some crisps for lunch, followed by a big bar of chocolate, and then I usually had sausage and chips at the college canteen in the evening. I didn't eat any fruit or vegetables. I started to feel tired all the time and my skin and hair looked awful. When I went home over the holidays my dad and my sisters were really shocked at my state of health. They spent every day over the next two weeks teaching me how to cook. I've learned that it is possible to cook great food even when you don't have much money. You don't have to buy many expensive ingredients. I get very little food from the supermarket – instead I buy fresh fruit and vegetables

from the local market, and I buy pasta, rice, lentils, kidney beans and other pulses online – you can get them really cheaply if you buy them in bulk. I love making stir fries in my wok or cooking some soup or stew. I like spicy food, and a little cumin can make a boring dish taste much better. Very few of my friends can cook as well as me, so I get a lot of visitors to my house at dinner time!

'For the competition, I created a traditional British menu. The starter was tomato and basil soup, followed by roast chicken with broccoli and roast potatoes. The dessert was a warm dark chocolate pudding with vanilla ice cream.'

2 Comprehension

Read about James again and answer these questions.

1 How many snack bars did he usually eat for breakfast in his first term?
2 How much fruit did he eat in his first term?
3 Is it necessary to have a lot of money if you want to cook well?
4 How much food does he now buy from the supermarket?
5 How does he improve the taste of a boring dish?

3 Vocabulary

a Use words from the article to label the pictures.

b Find at least two food items in the article for each category.

herbs & spices
meat
pulses
vegetables
carbohydrates

c Can you think of one more word for each category?

Grammar spot
Countable and uncountable nouns review

Look at the examples below and choose the correct option to complete the rules.

We use **much** and **(a) little** with *countable/uncountable* nouns.
We use **many** and **(a) few** with *countable/uncountable* nouns.
We use **some**, **any**, **a lot of (lots of)** with *countable nouns/both countable and uncountable nouns*.

It is possible to cook good food even when you don't have **much money**.
A little cumin can make a boring dish taste much better.
Very **few** of my **friends** can cook as well as me.
You don't have to buy **many** expensive **ingredients**.
I get **a lot of visitors**.
I spent **a lot of time**.

Grammar page 97

4 Grammar practice

Choose the correct option to complete the text.

James takes us on a tour of his student kitchen.

It's nearly the end of term now, so I've only got ¹ _____ money left to last me until I go home for the holidays. You'll see that there's ² _____ of very cheap food: potatoes, lentils and ³ _____ tins of beans, but there aren't ⁴ _____ luxuries here! I've only got ⁵ _____ of saucepans and a wok. You don't need ⁶ _____ expensive equipment to start cooking. I love herbs and spices, though, so I've got ⁷ _____ jars of spices! And I'm also growing ⁸ _____ pots of fresh herbs on the balcony.

	a		**b**		**c**	
1	a	few	b	much	c	a little
2	a	many	b	a lot	c	any
3	a	some	b	a couple	c	much
4	a	much	b	few	c	any
5	a	a couple	b	few	c	little
6	a	lots	b	a few	c	much
7	a	a little	b	lots of	c	any
8	a	a few	b	a little	c	much

5 Speaking

Work with a classmate. Turn to page 87 and look at the three pictures. Take it in turns to describe one of the pictures.

6 Listening and writing

a [2.12] Rob is describing one of his favourite recipes. Listen and put the instructions into the correct order.

a Fry the mushrooms.
b Mix the eggs, milk and salt.
c Add the ham and mushrooms.
d Pour the egg and milk mixture into the pan.
e Fold the omelette and tip it onto a plate.
f Chop up the ham and mushrooms.
g Take the mushrooms out of the pan.

b Write instructions on how to prepare one of your favourite meals. Try to include these verbs: *mix, chop, pour, add, fry.*

My favourite dish is onion soup. You need five or six onions, some garlic, some stock ...

7 Check your English

Rewrite these sentences using the word in brackets.

1 I don't have much bread in the cupboard.

1 I don't have a lot of bread in the cupboard. (much)
I don't have _____.
2 There aren't many bananas in the bowl. (few)
There are only _____.
3 There are no grapes in my lunchbox. (any)
I don't have _____.
4 I haven't got much money. (little)
I've only got _____.
5 There are two onions on the table. (couple)
There are _____.
6 There are only a few carrots on your plate. (many)
There aren't _____.

18 I'm in trouble!

1 Presentation

a Work with a classmate. Look at the photo and discuss the questions.

1 What is Marija doing?
2 Does she look happy or unhappy?

b ⟦2.13⟧ Listen and read Marija and Janiki's dialogue. Check your answers to Part a.

Janiki Hi Marija, it's Janiki!

Marija Oh hi Janiki. Where are you?

Janiki I'm at home. I'm on my own at the moment but Rob will be here in a minute. We're going to cycle to Cannon Hill Park. There's an open-air concert there this afternoon. Why don't you join us?

Marija I don't think I can. My mum's making me tidy my room and she won't let me go out until I've finished.

Janiki No way! Can't you do it later?

Marija No. I'm in a lot of trouble right now. I borrowed my mum's jacket for a party last week and now I can't find it because my room's in a mess.

Janiki Your mum lets you borrow her clothes? You're lucky! My mum never lets me use her stuff. Well … I don't actually want to wear any of my mum's clothes. But I wish I could borrow her hair straighteners sometimes.

Marija Well, she won't let me borrow her stuff anymore. It's so unfair! And when I've finished this, I've got to clear out the cupboard under the stairs, where I keep all my sewing things. Honestly, she's in such a bad mood today!

Janiki Hmm. Well, at least your dad doesn't make you clean the car every weekend. That is the most boring job ever.

Marija Yes, but that's because we don't have a car, Janiki! Anyway, look Harry's on his way here at the moment. Maybe he can help me. I don't want to stay at home all day.

Janiki Well, hurry up! The concert starts at half past three and we want to get there on time so that we don't miss the main act.

Real English

- No way!
- You're lucky.
- It's so unfair!
- Honestly
- Hurry up!

2 Comprehension

Read the dialogue again and answer these questions.

1 Where is Janiki?
2 Why do Janiki and Rob want to go to Cannon Hill Park?
3 Why is Marija in trouble?
4 What does Marija have to do?
5 Who is in a bad mood?
6 Who has to clean the car every weekend?
7 Who is going to Marija's house?
8 Why does Janiki say, 'Hurry up!'?

Grammar spot
Make / let + object + infinitive without *to*

After the verbs *let* and *make*, we use an object and infinitive without *to*.

Complete the sentences with words from the dialogue.

1 My mum's **making** _____.
2 Your dad doesn't **make** _____.
3 Your mum **lets** _____.
4 She won't **let** _____.

3 Grammar practice

Choose the correct option.

1 My teacher doesn't *make/let* us do homework every night.
2 My dad *makes/lets* me watch TV when I come home from school.
3 My mum doesn't *make/let* me drink coffee after six in the evening.
4 My sister *made/let* me borrow her boots.
5 My parents won't *make/let* me go to the party tonight.
6 Our school *makes/lets* us wear school uniform.

4 Speaking and writing

a Complete this chart about yourself. Then use *let* and *make* to tell a classmate about your family rules.

Household Rules

Do you have to take the rubbish out?		Yes/No
Do you have to tidy your room every weekend?		Yes/No
Do you have to help prepare the meals at home?		Yes/No
Are you allowed to stay up late at weekends?		Yes/No
Are you allowed to borrow your parents' stuff?		Yes/No
Are you allowed to wear shoes in the house?		Yes/No

> *My parents don't make me take the rubbish out.*

b Use *make* and *let* to write four more sentences about rules in your house. Write two true and two false sentences.

c Read your sentences to your partner. Can he/she guess the false sentences?

5 Pronunciation

a Write these words from the dialogue under the correct sound, /əʊ/ or /ɒ/.

> open concert want clothes
> honestly home own got

/əʊ/	/ɒ/
open	*concert*

b [2.14] Now listen and check your answers.

6 Vocabulary

a Find these phrases in the dialogue then complete them with *on* or *in*.

1 ____ a mess
2 ____ time
3 ____ a bad mood
4 ____ my own
5 ____ his way
6 ____ a lot of trouble

b Use phrases from Part a to complete these questions.

1 What makes you happy and what puts you _____?
2 What things do you like doing _____ and what do you like doing with other people?
3 Is your room often _____ or is it always tidy?
4 Are you usually _____ for school or are you sometimes late?
5 Have you ever been _____ at home or are you always very good?

c Discuss your answers to the questions with a classmate.

Study tip

Collocations
A collocation is two or more words that often go together. Some examples are:
preposition + noun (*in a mess*)
adjective + noun (*rich food*)
verb + noun (*make your bed*)
Keep a list of common collocations and make up your own tests to revise them regularly.

7 Song

[2.15] Find the song *Keep on* on page 85.

8 Check your English

Put the words in order to make sentences.

1 sister/really/mood/today/My/in/a/bad/is
2 lets/play/dad/my/never/console/me/games/My/on
3 teacher/us/makes/English/class/Our/in/speak
4 is/My/lot/trouble/in/dog/of/a
5 in/bed/mum/lets/11/Saturdays/her/stay/until/Tina's/on

19 Sell, sell, sell

1 Presentation

a Look at the pictures below. What products do you think they are advertising? Discuss your ideas with a classmate.

perfume   tourism   vitamins   cars   health food
beauty products   energy (e.g. electricity or gas)

b (2.16) Listen and read and check your ideas.

What's behind a picture?

Victor Scardino is the Creative Director of WhiteRedYellow – one of the most successful advertising agencies in the world. He tells us about his favourite advertisements and explains the theory behind the image.

An advertisement is so much more than a picture with some words. A good advertisement not only tries to sell a product, it also tries to make you feel an emotion. It might try to create a whole new world for you – a world which you, the consumer, will want to be part of.

Advertisers can create this world in many different ways. Sometimes they use pictures of celebrities with their products. The choice of celebrity is very important, because he or she gives out a message about the product. If the celebrity is an actor from a popular soap opera, for example, the message is that the product is safe, familiar, part of our everyday lives. If the celebrity is a Hollywood actor, then the message is that the product is glamorous and exciting.

But for me, personally, the most interesting advertisements are the ones which make you think. You look and you don't immediately know what the product is.

Here's an example of one of my favourite advertisements. It's a giant ape, holding his foot. In front of the ape is the city skyline. It could be an advertisement for a film – of course it looks a lot like the classic film *King Kong*. It might be an advertisement for a city. But look more carefully, and you see that the ape is in pain. His foot must hurt. And now you read the tagline, 'Small but tough,' and, of course, you recognise the familiar Volkswagen logo. So this is an advertisement for a small car. How do you feel now? You may laugh because it's a funny image. You could feel quite clever because you've understood the joke. You probably thought about the film *King Kong* – a classic film. So you are filled with good emotions and you associate the Volkswagen brand with all these positive feelings.

This is another great advertisement. It shows an elderly woman, smiling. She looks happy and healthy, but her skin is very wrinkled. Surely this can't be an advertisement for a beauty product? But yes, it is. Dove, a beauty product company, used this advertisement as part of its 'Campaign for Real Beauty'. In this campaign they didn't use slim, glamorous models, they used pictures of many different ordinary women. Their campaign sends out the message that Dove understands and appreciates all different types of women. It says that there are lots of different ways of being beautiful. Dove increased their sales by 700% when this advertisement first appeared.

Small but tough. Polo.

□ wrinkled?
□ wonderful?

2 Vocabulary

a Work with a classmate. Find these words in the article. Can you guess what they mean?

logo   tagline   product   brand
consumer   campaign

b Work in small groups. Try to think of:

- two taglines from recent advertisements
- the logos for three different car companies
- four products you have bought in the last month.

Compare your ideas with other groups.

3 Comprehension

Read the article again. Are these sentences true (T) or false (F)?

1 A good advertisement will try to do more than just sell the product.
2 Advertisements use TV actors because they want the products to seem glamorous and exciting.
3 In the Volkswagen advertisement, it is immediately obvious that the product is a car.
4 The Volkswagen advertisement creates many positive associations with their brand.
5 It is unusual to use a picture of an old woman in an advertisement for a beauty product.
6 Dove's 'Campaign for Real Beauty' was not very successful.

Grammar spot
Modals of speculation and deduction: *could, may/might, can't* and *must*

Look at the examples below and complete the rules with *could, may/might, can't* and *must.*

a We use _____ and _____ to talk about things which are possible but not certain.
b We use _____ to talk about things we believe aren't true.
c We use _____ to talk about things we believe are true.

1 His foot **must** hurt.
2 It **could** be an advertisement for a film or it **might** be an advertisement for a city.
3 This **can't** be an advertisement for a beauty product.

Note that we use *could, may/might, can't* and *must* with an infinitive without *to.*

Grammar page 98

4 Grammar practice

Complete the second sentence with *may/might, must* or *can't* so it means the same as the first sentence.

Where's my bag?

1 It might be under my bed.

1 I think perhaps it's under my bed.
It _____ under my bed.
2 No, it's not there. Well, maybe it's in the cupboard downstairs.
It _____ in the cupboard downstairs.
3 It's definitely not in the kitchen because I've already looked there.
It _____ in the kitchen because I've already looked there.
4 Mum probably knows where it is.
Mum _____ where it is.
5 What's that noise?
It's my phone. And my phone's in my bag.
So my bag is definitely in this room!
My bag _____ in this room!

5 Speaking

a Work with a classmate. Look at the two advertisements on page 88. What products are they advertising? Why are they using these images? Discuss your ideas using *could, may, might, can't* and *must.*

It could be an advertisement for glasses, because his eyes look strange.

It can't be an advertisement for shampoo because he doesn't have much hair!

b **Student A** Turn to page 86 to find out about Advertisement A.
Student B Turn to page 89 to find out about Advertisement B.

6 Writing

Work with a classmate. Choose one of these products.

a perfume   a snack bar   a watch
a mobile phone   a car

Design an advertisement for your product. Think about these things.

- What is your target market? What kind of people will be interested in this product?
- What message do you want to give the consumer?
- Do you want your advertisement to be funny/glamorous/dangerous/safe?
- Think of a tagline for your advertisement.
- Use a photo from a magazine or draw a picture to illustrate your advertisement.

7 Check your English

Make sentences with *could, may/might, must* and *can't* about these situations.

1 I've switched on the TV but there's no picture on the screen.
must / be / broken
2 I can hear a strange noise from the garden.
could / be / a fox
3 Who's that boy with the red hair?
can't / be / James / because / have / blond hair
4 Where's your coat?
might / be / in the car / or / could / be / at Tom's house
5 Look! There's a ghost at the window!
can't / be / a ghost / must / be / your little brother

Skills

Hot Spot

Out and about in town

In this week's issue, we review our five favourite places in town to relax, eat some good food, and meet your friends.

The Jumping Bean

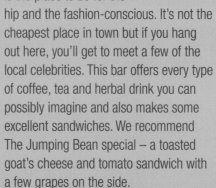

This chic, modern coffee bar in the centre of town is the place to be for the hip and the fashion-conscious. It's not the cheapest place in town but if you hang out here, you'll get to meet a few of the local celebrities. This bar offers every type of coffee, tea and herbal drink you can possibly imagine and also makes some excellent sandwiches. We recommend The Jumping Bean special – a toasted goat's cheese and tomato sandwich with a few grapes on the side.

The Blue Fox Café

It's loud and it's lively. The Blue Fox Café is always crowded and the music is very, very loud, so don't come here if you're looking for a little quiet conversation! The chicken salad sandwiches are famous – and still only £2.50 for a sandwich and a cup of strong tea – a real bargain! You'll love the comfortable old sofas and you can spend hours looking at all the music posters on the walls. Their coffee is rather weak and they don't offer much food for vegetarians, but the atmosphere is amazing.

The Crocus Tea Rooms

This place must have looked exactly the same thirty years ago. It offers a fantastic range of cakes and pastries, and you can enjoy the food at pretty tables, with floral tablecloths and lots of vases of fresh flowers. There's always relaxing classical music in the background and we think this is a great place to take your granny! Try a slice of their tasty lemon cake or an old-fashioned fruit scone and enjoy the calm, peaceful surroundings.

Make-a-Shake

You won't get coffee or tea here, and you won't even be able to get a sandwich, because at Make-a-Shake they make lots of milkshakes and that's all. But what an amazing range! They offer over 28 different types of milkshake, from strawberry and apple to mint, chocolate and blueberry. You can choose the ingredients yourself and then watch the staff blend them with milk and ice cream to make a delicious milkshake. Our favourite is toffee and banana – not very healthy but great fun!

Asparagus

This is possibly the healthiest café in town and it's full of very serious, healthy people! It's not very trendy or modern, but all the food is organic and also delicious. They have a big range of salads and vegetarian dishes and there are also lots of different types of fruit juices available. We recommend the lentil and mushroom bake with a big glass of carrot juice. (Then you can pop across the road to Make-a-Shake and have a huge chocolate milkshake!)

1 Reading

a Read the reviews and match each person with a place.

1 Greta loves making up her own recipes and experimenting with different flavours. She loves sweet drinks.

2 Milly loves going to the most stylish places in town. She doesn't eat meat and she doesn't like unhealthy food.

3 Joe loves traditional cakes and wants to go somewhere with a quiet, relaxing atmosphere.

4 Toby hasn't got much money and is looking for a café where he can relax with his friends and listen to some great music.

b Find words and phrases in the reviews that mean the same as these words.

1 very good value
2 trendy
3 full of activity
4 delicious
5 mix together
6 go somewhere quickly

2 Writing

Imagine your ideal café and write a review for the magazine. Write about 80 words. Include information about these things:

- the kind of food and drink available
- how the place looks
- what kind of people go there
- your favourite meal/drink there.

Hot Spot

"Quiz Time"

Now it's time for our quiz podcast! We went out and about and met some of our readers. But can you guess what they're talking about? Listen carefully!

The first correct entry wins a year's free subscription to Hot Spot Magazine.

3 Listening

2.17 Listen to the quiz and choose the correct answer A, B or C.

1 What are the girls going to do?

A

B

C

2 Where do the boys want to go?

A
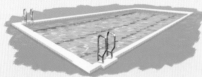
B

C

3 What has the man bought?

A

B

C

4 What time does the train leave?

A

B

C

Noughts and crosses

Work with a classmate or in small groups. One person/group draws noughts (O). The other person/group draws crosses (X).

Pick a square and complete the sentence in the square with your own ideas. If your sentence is correct, you can put a nought/cross in the square.

The first person/group to make a line is the winner.

There are a few …	My teacher makes us …	We haven't got any …
My brother lets me …	How many …	My mum doesn't let me …
We've got a little …	My parents don't make me …	How much …

Review

Check you can do these things.

1 I can talk about quantity.

Choose the correct option (A, B, C or D) to complete each gap.

I don't have ¹ _____ time at the moment because I'm studying for my exams. I have to finish a couple ² _____ projects this weekend, and I want to find out ³ _____ information about volcanoes for my geography coursework. It's difficult to study at home because there's only a ⁴ _____ space in our house and there are a ⁵ _____ of people in my family! Tomorrow I'm going to go to the library in town to study. It's very quiet and there aren't ⁶ _____ people there on Saturday afternoons. When my exams are over and the holidays begin, I'm going to spend ⁷ _____ day at the beach! I live very close to the sea and ⁸ _____ my friends meet up at the beach during the holidays. It will be fantastic!

1	**A**	many	**B**	much	**C**	few	**D** lot
2	**A**	of	**B**	for	**C**	the	**D** in
3	**A**	a few	**B**	a couple of	**C**	many	**D** some
4	**A**	little	**B**	much	**C**	lot	**D** couple
5	**A**	lots	**B**	lot	**C**	many	**D** some
6	**A**	a lot	**B**	every	**C**	much	**D** many
7	**A**	a few	**B**	a little	**C**	any	**D** every
8	**A**	a couple	**B**	lots of	**C**	a lot	**D** many

2 I know vocabulary for food.

Find twelve food words in the grid and use them to label the pictures below.

I	C	E	C	R	E	A	M	B	O	B
P	A	T	H	L	E	T	R	R	T	O
A	H	E	M	U	S	H	R	O	O	M
S	C	H	I	C	K	E	N	C	M	R
T	R	A	L	T	E	A	R	C	A	I
A	E	M	K	W	S	V	K	O	T	C
B	U	T	T	E	R	C	P	L	O	E
A	B	R	E	A	D	C	H	I	P	S

1 _____

2 _____

3 _____

4 _____

5 _____

6 _____

7 _____

8 _____

9 _____

10 _____

11 _____

12 _____

3 I can use *make* and *let* to talk about permission and obligation.

Use the prompts to write sentences in the present simple.

1 My dad/make/my sister/tidy her room/every weekend
2 My teacher/not let/us/bring our mobile phones/into the classroom
3 Sophie/sometimes/let/her friend/borrow/her favourite boots
4 your parents/let/you/ride a scooter?
5 My friend/not let/me/read her e-mails
6 Our school/not make/us/wear a school uniform

4 I know six noun phrases with *in* and *on*.

Choose the correct option for each sentence.

1 Your room is *in/on* a mess. Please tidy it up!
2 I'm never *in/on* time for school.
3 My sister is *in/on* trouble because she stayed out late last night.
4 Don't talk to James! He's *in/on* a really bad mood.
5 Harry just phoned. He's *in/on* his way here now.
6 I don't want to go to Stacey's party *in/on* my own. Please come with me.

5 I can use *could*, *may/might*, *must* and *can't* to make speculations and deductions.

a Complete the sentence with *must* or *can't*.

1 Sarah's not in the kitchen but her coat and bag are here. She _____ be in her bedroom.
2 You _____ be Leo's brother. Leo hasn't got a brother.
3 My laptop _____ be in your office because it's on the table in front of me!
4 There's no picture on the TV screen. It _____ be broken.
5 Ferdi _____ be on holiday at the moment. He's not replying to his phone calls.
6 It _____ be true. I don't believe it.

b Use *may/might* or *could* to speculate about these things.

It might be …

It could be …

6 Now use the language from Module 5 to complete this activity.

Complete the second sentence so that it means the same as the first sentence. Use 1–3 words.

1 There's only a little rice in the packet.
   There isn't _____ rice in the packet.
2 I haven't got many friends.
   I've only got _____ friends.
3 At home I have to prepare supper every night.
   My parents _____ me prepare supper every night.
4 At our school we can't run in the corridors.
   Our school doesn't _____ us run in the corridors.
5 Katie is coming to the party now.
   Katie is on _____ to the party now.

Extra special

Mini play

a **[2.18]** Listen and read. Does Jenny like shopping? Does Steve like shopping?

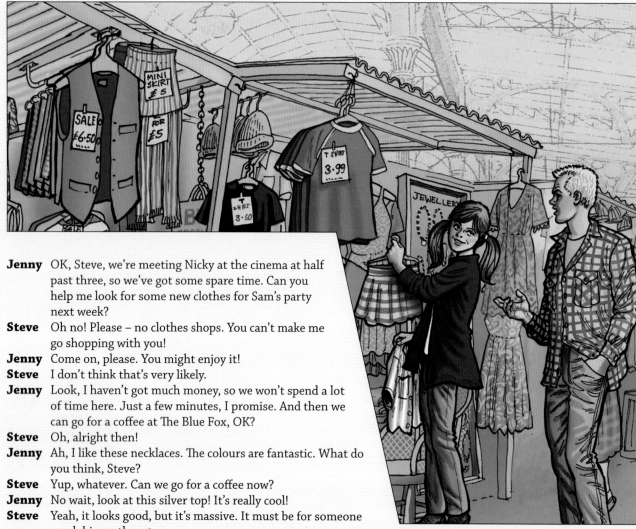

Jenny OK, Steve, we're meeting Nicky at the cinema at half past three, so we've got some spare time. Can you help me look for some new clothes for Sam's party next week?

Steve Oh no! Please – no clothes shops. You can't make me go shopping with you!

Jenny Come on, please. You might enjoy it!

Steve I don't think that's very likely.

Jenny Look, I haven't got much money, so we won't spend a lot of time here. Just a few minutes, I promise. And then we can go for a coffee at The Blue Fox, OK?

Steve Oh, alright then!

Jenny Ah, I like these necklaces. The colours are fantastic. What do you think, Steve?

Steve Yup, whatever. Can we go for a coffee now?

Jenny No wait, look at this silver top! It's really cool!

Steve Yeah, it looks good, but it's massive. It must be for someone much bigger than you.

Jenny Well, it might be but I still really love it. And I can wear it with a big belt. Now, are there any interesting skirts here?

Steve Hmm, I can't really see many skirts. There are lots of dresses, but not many skirts. What kind of thing are you looking for?

Jenny Um, I don't know exactly. Just something a bit unusual. How about this stripy mini skirt?

Steve No way! That's really horrible.

Jenny Oh. OK, fair enough. Right, well I'll get the silver top and this pink necklace. Good, that's it. That only took five minutes.

Steve Oh, hang on, come over here, Jenny. What do you think of this blue waistcoat?

Jenny Well, I'm not sure really. I don't usually wear blue. It doesn't suit me.

Steve Not for you, for me! It would look great with my jeans. It's only £6.50 and it looks amazing. I'm going to try it on.

Jenny Um, OK. So, you do like clothes shops, then.

Steve No, I don't. I hate shopping. I just want to try on this waistcoat. Oh, and maybe that T-shirt. The black one.

b [2.19] Now listen and read the last part of the play. Who likes shopping now? Who hates shopping?

[one hour later]

Steve   Oh, and look over there. They've got lots of amazing hats! I want to try on a hat.

Jenny   Oh, come on, Steve. I'm really bored. We've been here for an hour. I want to go to the café. I hate shopping!

Steve   Yup, just let me look over there. There are a few interesting scarves in that box. I really like the purple ones.

Jenny   Aagggghh!

Memory challenge

Learn your lines by heart.

Mini project

1   Read Jem's review of his favourite film. Which things does he mention?

> the plot
>
> the acting
>
> the special effects
>
> the lighting
>
> the costumes
>
> the score

My favourite film is 'Avatar'. The special effects were amazing and it was incredible to see how the film-makers had created a completely new and very beautiful world with a whole new species. I loved the music and I thought it went very well with the action of the film. I also really liked the environmental message that came from the film. The acting was superb, especially Sigourney Weaver as Grace. My only criticism is that I think the film was slightly too long.

Jem

2   Now write a review of your favourite film. Write between 80–100 words. Try to mention at least four of the features listed above.

21 First impressions

1 Presentation

a [2.20] Look at the people in the picture. Listen and read. Is everyone following the tips in *Watch your body language*?

b [2.21] Look at the picture again. Listen to the dialogue. Which boy and girl are speaking?

Getting to know you

It only takes us a few seconds to form an opinion of someone. We look at the person's appearance and body language, listen to their first words and decide if we want to continue to talk to them or not. First impressions are important so read these tips on meeting someone for the first time.

Keep the conversation flowing
- Greet the other person.
- Introduce yourself.
- Find out the other person's name and use their name in the conversation.
- A good way to start the conversation is to talk about something around you or talk about people you both know.
- Compliment the other person about something.
- Ask their opinion about something.
- Show you are interested in what they say.
- Find out about the other person.
- Don't talk about anything controversial or too personal.
- Don't talk too much about yourself.

Watch your body language
- Look friendly and smile.
- Don't keep your arms folded.
- Look confident and try not to look nervous.
- Look the other person in the eyes, but don't stare!
- Don't stand too close to the other person.

c [2.21] Listen to the dialogue again. Work through the tips in *Keep the conversation flowing*. Did Mel and Craig do all the things?

Greet the other person — Yes, they did.

2 Comprehension

[2.21] Listen to the dialogue again. Are these sentences true (T) or false (F)? Correct the false sentences.

1 Craig asked Mel what her name was.
2 Mel said that she knew Craig's sister.
3 Craig asked Mel where she knew his sister from.
4 Mel told Craig she was in the same class as his sister.
5 Craig said his sister was at the party.
6 Craig asked Mel where she had bought her sunglasses.
7 Mel told Craig she didn't like Keane.
8 Craig asked Mel if she was interested in sunglasses.
9 Mel said she played in a band.
10 Mel asked Craig to pass her coat.
11 Mel told Craig to look the band up on Facebook®.

3 Vocabulary

Find the words in bold in the text on page 70. Then answer the questions.

1 What was your **first impression** of your best friend?
2 Do you **form** an opinion of people quickly?
3 What do you usually say when you **greet** someone?
4 What do you say when you want to **introduce** yourself?
5 Has anybody **complimented** you recently?
6 What things do you find **controversial**?
7 Can you look **confident**?
8 Can you look **nervous**?

Grammar spot
Direct speech / Reported speech review

Read the examples then answer the questions.

Direct speech	Reported speech
'I know your sister.'	Mel said she knew Craig's sister.
'I like your sunglasses.'	Craig told Mel he liked her sunglasses.
'Where did you get them?'	Craig asked Mel where she had got them.
'Are you into music?'	Craig asked if Mel was into music.
'Can you pass me my bag?'	Mel asked Craig to pass him her bag.
'Look us up on Facebook.'	Mel told Craig to look them up on Facebook.

1 Which form changes the tense?
2 Which form uses past reporting verbs?
3 Which form uses question marks?
4 Which form uses the exact words people say?

Grammar page 99

4 Grammar practice

You hear classmates say these things at school. Report what they said.

1 She said she was hungry.

1 'I'm hungry.' → She said she _____ hungry.
2 'Has anyone seen my book?' → He asked if anyone _____ his book.
3 'I don't like physics.' → She told him she _____ physics.
4 'I've forgotten my homework.' → He said he _____ his homework.
5 'Can you hold my bag?' → She asked if he _____ her bag.
6 'Don't speak to me.' → He told them not _____ him.
7 'Where are you going?' → She asked him where he _____.
8 'I'm going to the gym.' → He said he _____ to the gym.

5 Speaking

a Memory game

Think of a few sentences about yourself.

I like chocolate.
I saw a good film at the weekend.
My telephone number is 759023.

b Play the game. Take it in turns to remember what was said and tell the next student your sentence.

Sam: *I like chocolate.*

Tess: *Sam said he liked chocolate. I saw a good film at the weekend.*

George: *Tess said she'd seen a good film at the weekend. My telephone number is 759023 …*

6 Writing

a Read the instructions.

- Write a list of the people you've spoken to this week.
- Make notes about what they said or asked you and what you said to them.
- Ask your teacher or use your dictionary for help with vocabulary.

my dentist – filling
my father – change wheels on our car
my best friend – lend him my bike
my maths teacher – a test on Friday
my little brother – stop coming into my room

b Now write a report about what you and the people said and asked. Then show a classmate your report.

Last Tuesday – I went to the dentist. My dentist told me that I had to have a filling. Last weekend – My father asked me to help him change the wheels on our car. I told my little brother to stop coming into my room.

7 Check your English

Report the sentences.

1 'Switch off the TV.' He told me …
2 'Where are you going?' She asked me …
3 'Did you sleep well?' He asked me …
4 'I can't swim.' She said she …
5 'Do you like sport?' He asked me …
6 'Can you pass me the book?' She asked me …
7 'I haven't got the money.' He said he …

71

22 Life without a ...

1 Presentation

a ⟨2.22⟩ Listen and read the online discussion. Who do you agree with most?

Blogz	Join Blogz Take a tour Search Blogz 🔍	
	Could you live without a mobile phone?	
	OK, I want to chat about mobile phones. I have one but I hardly ever use it. It just sits on my desk at home and is switched off most of the time. So I believe I could live without a mobile phone.	
	What! Are you crazy, Owl? I don't agree at all. I definitely couldn't live without my mobile. Someone's always texting or calling me to find out where I am …	
	I agree, Sun. Nor could I. My phone's my best friend. I've got all my numbers on it. I take pictures with it. I use it as an alarm to wake me up in the morning … I don't think I could live without it.	
	I'm sorry, Cloud, but I don't agree. I think you're addicted to your phones! OK, I agree a mobile phone can be useful, but I don't believe you couldn't live without one. We've only had mobiles for about 20 years. Before that people lived for hundreds of thousands of years without them.	
	Yes, but did they have a social life? 🙂	
	🙂 Good one, Cloud!	
	I think it's people with mobile phones who don't have a social life. They're too busy taking calls to speak to anyone properly. I just hate it. You're talking to someone, their phone rings and they stop talking to you! Why don't they tell the other person to call back? I think that's so rude.	
	So do I. And I think it's really bad that some people have their ring tone set really loud …	
	That's right. I agree absolutely. Thanks for joining in, Doc.	
	I'm sorry, but I don't agree with you, Doc. I believe it's all about what kind of person you are. If you've got lots of friends, then you love your phone. If you're an anti-social type with no friends, then you don't need one.	
	What! 😠 That's rubbish. I've got lots of friends, real friends, people I meet and talk to face to face – not just people you call on your mobile and say 'What're you doing?' I don't believe you need a mobile to have friends.	
	You're right. Nor do I. 🙂	
	I lost my phone a couple of weeks ago and didn't have one for two whole days. I was lost. I just couldn't live without it …	
	That's right. And hey Owl! What about if you were in an emergency situation? Wouldn't you use your phone then? Mobile phones have saved people's lives …	
	I'm not saying they're not useful sometimes, I'm just saying people use them too much.	

b Read the text again. Who thinks they could live without a mobile phone?

2 Vocabulary and speaking

Find the words in bold in the text. Then answer the questions about yourself.

1 What are you **addicted** to?
2 Do you think it is good to have mobile phone **ring tones** set really **loud**?
3 Do you use an **alarm** to wake up in the morning?
4 Do you think of yourself as an **anti-social** type of person?
5 Do you prefer **chatting** to friends on the phone or **face to face**?
6 Have you ever been in an **emergency situation**? What was it?
7 What is the most **useful** thing you've got?

Real English
- That's rubbish.
- That's right.
- Good one.

72

3 Comprehension

a Choose the correct words.

1 Owl *uses/doesn't use* her mobile phone a lot.
2 Cloud uses her mobile phone for *chatting and texting/ lots of things*.
3 People have had mobiles for *about 20 years/hundreds of thousands of years*.
4 Owl doesn't like it when people *don't answer/interrupt a conversation to answer* their mobile.
5 Owl thinks you *don't need/need* to have a mobile phone to have friends.
6 Cloud *hasn't got/has got* a mobile phone at the moment.

b Who do you agree with – Owl and Doc or Sun and Cloud?

Grammar spot
think and *believe*

When we use *think* and *believe* to give our opinion about something we never use the continuous.

I **think** it's people with mobile phones who don't have a social life.
I **don't think** I could live without it.
I **believe** I could definitely live without a mobile phone.
I **don't believe** that you couldn't live without one.

4 Writing

Work with a classmate. Read the instructions.

- Write some opinions on a sheet of paper using *we think* or *we believe*. Leave space under each opinion for your classmates to write comments.
- Pass the sheets of paper around the class.
- Write comments about your classmates' opinions.
- When you have finished, read your classmates' comments.

> We think snowboarding is the most exciting sport in the world.
>
> I'm sorry, but I don't agree. I think F1 racing is the most exciting sport.
>
> So do I.

Useful expressions

Agreeing and disagreeing with someone

That's right.   Nor do I.
I agree absolutely.   I'm sorry, but I don't think you're right.
So do I.   I'm sorry, but I don't agree.

5 Listening

a [2.23] Discuss this question with your classmates. What's your opinion?

What's the best place to watch a film – at home on TV or in the cinema?

Then listen to Rob and his friends. What do they think?

b [2.23] Listen again and answer the questions.

1 Where do the boys like watching films?
2 Where do the girls like watching films?
3 What do the girls like doing when they're watching a film?
4 When do the boys think you should talk about the film?
5 What kind of films do the boys think you have to watch in the cinema?
6 What do the girls think the big advantage of watching a film on DVD is?

Study tip

Before you do a listening activity and know the subject of what you are going to listen to, try to predict what you are going to hear.
For example: Watching films on TV or in the cinema?
Small screen/large screen, cheaper/more expensive, have to go out/can stay at home

6 Check your English

a Write four opinions using these expressions.

1 I think …   3 I believe …
2 I don't think … 4 I don't believe …

b Then tell your classmates your opinions. Agree or disagree with what you hear.

> I don't think exams are necessary.

> I don't agree. It's important to find out how much you know.

> I agree. I believe they are a waste of time.

23 Barbecue chat

1 Presentation

[2.24] Rob and his friends are at a barbecue at a new neighbour's house.
Listen and read. Which of these topics do they talk about?

sport   the food   pets   the weather   TV   nationality   school   music

Rob   Your name is Lance, isn't it?
Lance   Yes, that's right.
Rob   Oh, hi Lance. My name's Rob. You're
       American, aren't you?
Lance   How did you guess? It wasn't my accent,
       was it?
Rob   Well, yes it was. But I am right, aren't I?
Lance   Yes, you're right. I am American. And
       we haven't met before, have we?
Rob   No, we haven't. Pleased to meet you and
       thanks for inviting us to your barbecue.
Lance   You're welcome.

Janiki   Listen to this.
Marija   Umm. I like it. It's really cool, isn't it? Who is it?
Janiki   What! Listen again. Come on. You know who it
       is, don't you?
Marija   No, I don't.
Janiki   Really? I don't believe you. But you've heard
       this before, haven't you?
Marija   No, I haven't. Honestly.
Janiki   You aren't kidding me, are you?
Marija   No, I'm not. I don't know who it is. Tell me.
       Who is it?

Harry   You're a vegetarian, aren't you?
Rachel   Yes, I am. How did you know? And you
       aren't a vegetarian, are you?
Harry   No, I'm not – as you can see. I love meat –
       especially chicken. The food isn't bad
       though, is it?
Rachel   No, it's great. It was really nice of Lance to
       invite us. Have you met Lance's parents yet?
Harry   Yes, I have. They're really nice, aren't they?
Rachel   Yes, they are. Really nice.

2 Comprehension

Read the dialogues again. Are these sentences true (T) or false (F)?

1   Lance is American.
2   Lance and Rob have met before.
3   Janiki doesn't believe Marija hasn't heard the song before.
4   Marija hasn't heard the song before.
5   Rachel is a vegetarian.
6   Harry hasn't met Lance's parents.

Real English

- Pleased to meet you.
- It's cool, isn't it?
- Honestly.
- You're not kidding me, are you?

Grammar spot
Tag questions

We often use tag questions to check if something is true or to ask someone to agree with us.
Look at how we form tag questions:

Affirmative **sentence**   Negative **tag**
    You are American,   aren't you?

    Negative **sentence**   Affirmative **tag**
We **haven't** met before,   **have** we?

Complete the questions.
1 Your name is Lance, ____?
2 It ____ really cool, isn't it?
3 It wasn't my accent, ____?
4 You ____ kidding me, are you?

Notice that we use short answers to answer tag questions.
You **aren't** a vegetarian, **are** you? **Yes, I am. / No, I'm not.**

Grammar page 100

3 Grammar practice

Complete the sentences with the correct question tag.

isn't it? haven't you? have we?
don't you? was she? is it?

1 She wasn't late, …
2 You've seen this film before, …
3 This programme is really interesting, …
4 You want to come with us, …
5 We haven't eaten there before, …
6 The food isn't very good, …

4 Pronunciation

a [2.25] Listen to two questions.

1 You're American,
    ↘
   aren't you?

   When we are sure of the answer and are asking someone to agree with us, we use a falling intonation.

2 Your name is
    ↗
   Lance, isn't it?

   When we are not sure of the answer and are checking that something is true, we use a rising intonation.

b [2.26] Listen. Is the intonation rising or falling? Then listen again and practise asking the questions.

1 It's really cool, isn't it?
2 But I am right, aren't I?
3 You're a vegetarian, aren't you?
4 The food isn't bad though, is it?
5 We haven't met before, have we?
6 You know who it is, don't you?
7 You aren't kidding me, are you?
8 They're really nice, aren't they?

5 Writing and speaking

a Choose a classmate you know well. Write five tag questions about things you know about him or her.

You live near the school, don't you?
You're 15, aren't you?
You don't like maths, do you?
You've got two brothers, haven't you?
You didn't come to school last Friday, did you?

b Practise asking your questions using a falling intonation.

c Ask and answer with your classmate. Use short answers.

You live near the school, don't you?

Yes, I do.

6 Listening

a [2.27] Marija meets someone she thinks she knows. Listen and complete the tag questions.

1 Hey, I know you, …
2 Your name's Marija, …
3 And you're Jason, …
4 We met at Janiki's birthday party, …
5 Yes, we did. When was that? It was last March, …
6 You go to Fairlight College, …
7 You don't like sport, …

b [2.27] Listen again. Practise saying the question tags with a rising intonation.

7 Check your English

Choose the correct word.

Dan I don't think we've met, *have/haven't* we?
Tim No, we haven't. Your name's Dan, *is/isn't* it?
Dan Yes, and you're Tim, *are/aren't* you?
Tim Yes, that's right. We met at Owen's party, *did/didn't* we?
Dan Yes, we did. You play in the same soccer team as Owen, *do/don't* you?
Tim Yes, that's right. And you don't play soccer, *do/don't* you?
Dan No, I play rugby. I don't think you like rugby, *do/don't* you?
Tim No, that's right. Not a lot.

Hot Spot

It's all about communicating
Can animals speak to us?

The answer to this question is no. No animal can communicate with human beings using spoken language. Chimpanzees can be taught sign language and then use it to communicate with human beings, but they can't use our spoken language. Their mouths and vocal organs are a different shape and can't make the same sounds as human beings. Parrots and a few other birds are the only animals that can talk like us. We can teach them some of our words and they can say them, but again they are not using our language to communicate with us. They just copy the sounds we make and then repeat it without any meaning.

But what about dogs? Dogs and human beings have lived together for thousands of years. They were our first pets even when we were nomads wandering around the world hunting and gathering food without any permanent home and are still used for hunting today. Surely, if there is any animal in the world that should talk like us, it is man's best friend, the domestic dog?

But again there is the problem with the shape of the mouth and vocal organs. They are not the same as ours and therefore can't say our words. But what dogs can do is bark. And that leads us to something very interesting. The ancestor of our pet dog, the wolf, doesn't communicate with other dogs by barking: it howls. So does the hyena and any other wild dog. So why does the domestic dog bark? Scientists now believe it is because they learnt to bark to communicate with us.

A bark is the only sound dogs can make in different ways. Most people who own a dog say their dog has different kinds of barks. Dog owners were played recordings of their pet's barks in scientific experiments and were able to identify what the different barks meant. 'That bark is when my dog wants me to open a door.' 'That bark is when I say, "Walk".' 'That bark is a sad bark.' 'That bark is happy.'

1 Reading

Read the text. Are these sentences true (T) or false (F)?

1 Chimpanzees can communicate with us but not with spoken language.
2 Chimpanzees have got the same shape mouth and vocal organs as human beings.
3 Parrots can say words like human beings.
4 Parrots don't use language to communicate with us.
5 Human beings didn't have dogs thousands of years ago.
6 Dogs can't say our words because of the shape of their mouths and vocal organs.
7 Wolves also bark to communicate with other wolves.
8 Most dog owners can understand what their dog's barks mean.

Hot Spot

"Five things I couldn't live without"

What five things couldn't you live without? These are the five things Jo Harvey couldn't live without. What do you think? Send us a text with a list of the five things you couldn't live without and tell us why.

1

2

3

4

5

2 Listening

a [2.28] Listen to Jo. Name the five things she couldn't live without.

b [2.28] Listen again and complete the sentences.

1 Jo spends a lot of time keeping her Facebook page _____.
2 She wants her Facebook page to be _____ and _____.
3 Jo says her mobile phone isn't the c_____ or the l_____.
4 She doesn't use her mobile to phone much because it is too _____.
5 She uses her mobile mainly for _____.
6 She texts all her friends _____.
7 Every evening she gets a lot of calls on her home phone from _____.
8 She makes a few calls on her home phone because it is _____.
9 Jo needs to listen to music _____.
10 She shares her music with her _____.

3 Writing

a Write a list of the five things you couldn't live without.

> 1 my family
> 2 my football boots
> 3 my bike
> 4 my best friends
> 5 my cat

b Write a paragraph about the five things.

The Contradiction Game

Play this game with a classmate. Decide who is Player A and who is Player B.

Player A turns to page 87 and 'serves' the statements to Player B.

Player B 'returns' the statement with short answers.

Player B scores 1 point for every correct 'return' he or she makes.

When Player A has finished, Player B turns to page 89 and 'serves' statements to Player A.

The winner is the player who has most points.

It's raining.

No, it isn't.

Correct. I haven't got any money.

Review

Check you can do these things.

1 I can report what someone said and asked.

Choose the correct word or words (A, B, C, D) to complete each gap.

Today started really badly when my mother [1] ____ me that she [2] ____ give me a lift to school. I phoned my friend Terry, and asked her [3] ____ I could get a lift with her, but she was already on the way to school. So I had to get the bus and got to school half an hour late. My teacher asked me [4] ____ I was late. She told me [5] ____ earlier in future. Then Mr Winters was really angry with us in maths. He said we [6] ____ the worst class in the school and told us we [7] ____ to work harder. But the afternoon was much better. Mrs Cartwright said she [8] ____ my history homework and Miss Johnstone [9] ____ me if I wanted to play for the softball team.

1	**A** said	**B** told	**C** asked	**D** tell
2	**A** couldn't	**B** can't	**C** can	**D** could
3	**A** where	**B** how	**C** who	**D** if
4	**A** if	**B** where	**C** when	**D** why
5	**A** to get up	**B** got up	**C** get up	**D** getting up
6	**A** was	**B** are	**C** were	**D** been
7	**A** had	**B** having	**C** have	**D** has
8	**A** liking	**B** like	**C** likes	**D** liked
9	**A** said	**B** asked	**C** told	**D** if

2 I can remember tips about body language and how to keep the conversation flowing when I meet someone for the first time.

Match the sentence halves.

1	Look	a	their name.
2	Don't keep	b	too much about yourself.
3	Try not to look	c	their opinion about something.
4	Don't stand	d	interested in what they say.
5	Greet	e	the other person about something.
6	Find out and use	f	friendly and smile.
7	Compliment	g	too close to the other person.
8	Ask	h	nervous.
9	Show you are	i	the other person.
10	Don't talk	j	your arms folded.

3 I can use *think* and *believe* to give opinions.

a Write sentences giving your true opinions with *I think, I don't think, I believe, I don't believe*.

1 happiness is more important than having lots of money
2 eating too many sweet things is bad for your health
3 talking to someone on the phone is better than face to face
4 snowboarding is cooler than skiing

b Work with a classmate. Take it in turns to tell each other your opinions and say if you agree or disagree. Use these phrases.

I'm sorry but I don't agree.   Nor do I.   That's right.
I'm sorry but I don't think you're right.
So do I.   I agree absolutely.

4 I can use tag questions to check information and get agreement.

a Complete the tag questions.

1 I know you, ____?
2 You aren't interested, ____?
3 You haven't got my keys, ____?
4 You can come to my party, ____?
5 You aren't meeting Chris today, ____?
6 You have played tennis before, ____?
7 You had breakfast this morning, ____?
8 You won't forget to phone me, ____?

b Read the situations and write tag questions.

1 You think the weather is beautiful today so you say to a neighbour:

It's …

3 You want to check if a friend is still coming to the cinema tonight so you ask:

You're still coming …

2 You want a friend to text you a phone number so you ask:

You couldn't …

4 You think a friend likes coffee, but you want to check if you are right so you ask:

You like …

5 Now use the language from Module 6 to complete this activity.

Complete the second sentence so that it means the same as the first sentence. Use 1–3 words.

1 'Tom, don't touch my things.'
   I told Tom _____ my things.
2 'Sally, where do you live?'
   I asked Sally _____ lived.
3 'Kelly, I can't lend you any money.'
   I told Kelly that I _____ any money.
4 I told my brother not to come into my room.
   I told my brother he _____ into my room.
5 I think you live near here.
   You live near here, _____?
6 I'm not sure I could live without it.
   I _____ I could live without it.

Extra special

Literature

1 Read the introduction. Use the picture to help you understand.

This extract is adapted from the 19th-century novel, *Oliver Twist* by Charles Dickens. It is the story of an orphan whose mother died when she was giving birth in a workhouse. England at the time was divided into parishes and each parish had a beadle who was a kind of policeman. Poor people who did not have homes or food to eat had to live in a workhouse. They were made to work very hard by the master of the workhouse and the food they were given there was very bad and was mainly gruel, a watery soup made out of oats.

2 〔2.29〕 Now listen and read.

Mr Bumble gave the orphan boy a name.

Mr Bumble was the parish beadle. He gave all the orphans names when they arrived at the workhouse. He named them using the letters of the alphabet. T was the next letter. So Mr Bumble named the child Twist – Oliver Twist.

Oliver was now eleven years old. He was a pale, thin child. All the workhouse children were thin and ill. They were always hungry.

The boys were fed three times a day. But all they got was a small bowl of gruel. Three small bowls of gruel were not enough. The hungry boys were desperate. They had a meeting and made a decision. One of them must ask for more food. All the boys looked at Oliver Twist.

Evening came. The boys stood in line in the long stone hall. They waited for their bowls of gruel. They ate very quickly. In a moment, every bowl was empty. All the boys looked at Oliver. He was also very hungry. Carrying his bowl, he walked up to the master of the workhouse. Oliver looked up at the man and spoke.

'Please, sir, I want some more,' he whispered.

'What did you say?' the master said in surprise.

'Please, sir, I want some more,' Oliver repeated.

The master gave a great shriek. He took hold of Oliver by the collar of his thin shirt.

'Get the beadle! Bring Mr Bumble here!' the master shouted in anger.

In a few minutes, Mr Bumble hurried in. He was a bad-tempered, big, fat man. He wore a big hat and carried a long thin stick.

'Well, what's the matter?' Mr Bumble asked angrily.

'Oliver Twist has asked for more!' the master cried.

'Asked for more?' Mr Bumble repeated. He glared at Oliver. 'He's asking us for more! This boy is bad, very bad. One day he'll be hanged. Give him to me!'

3 Read the story again and discuss your answers to these questions.

1 Who decided that Oliver must ask for more gruel?
2 Why were the master and the beadle so angry with Oliver?
3 Why was it better for Oliver to run away?

Then Mr Bumble got hold of Oliver. He beat the poor child with his stick. When the beadle was tired, he threw Oliver onto the ground.

'Lock the boy in the cellar!' he shouted. 'Then he must leave the workhouse. He will be sold as an apprentice.'

The next day a notice was put up outside the workhouse.

> PARISH BOY FOR SALE
> £5 will be paid to anyone who will take a parish boy as an apprentice

Oliver sat in the dark cellar. He was cold, hungry and afraid.

If I stay here, I'll die, he thought. But a new master may kill me. I'll run away!

The night was cold and dark. Oliver climbed carefully out of a small window. He hurried along the quiet streets.

There was a large stone outside the town. On the stone was written, LONDON – 10 MILES.

'Mr Bumble won't find me in London,' Oliver said to himself.

So Oliver started to walk.

Mini project

1 First read Max's questions for his dream interview. Then find the answers in the interview.

Dream Interview

Questions

1 Do you like living in the White House?
2 What do you like about your job?
3 How many countries have you visited?
4 How do you usually travel?
5 Were you a good student at school?
6 What was your best subject at school?

Interview

Last week I interviewed the President of the United States inside the Oval Office, the official office of the President. I began my interview by asking her if she liked living in the White House. She told me that she didn't like it very much because the White House was more a place to work than a home. Then I asked the President what she liked about her job. She said the best thing about the job was travelling to different countries and meeting lots of interesting people. Then I asked her how many countries she had visited and she told me she had been to twelve countries. I asked her how she usually travelled and she told me she usually flew to the airport in a helicopter and then flew on Air Force 1 – the President's special plane. I finished the interview by asking the President if she had been a good student at school and what had been her best school subject. She told me she hadn't been a very good student and her best subject had been sport.

Max

2 Choose a famous person (real or imaginary) and write six questions to ask him or her. Then write a report of the interview. Imagine how the person answers your questions.

3 Ask your classmates to read your interview and find the answers to the questions.

Exam spot 3

PET Reading Part 3

In Part 3 of the Reading Paper, you have to read a long factual text and answer ten true/false questions about the text.

Tip

Read the questions carefully and then scan the text to find the answers. The questions will always be in the same order as the information in the text.

1 Look at the sentences in Activity 2. Underline the parts of text that will help you to answer the questions.

WINDMILLS OF CHANGE

William Kamkwamba and the windmill he built

Today, William Kamkwamba is a student at the African Leadership Academy in South Africa. Although he's only in his twenties, he's already written a book and he's given a lecture at a technology conference in the USA. But just a few years ago, in 2001, William had to leave school when he was 14 years old, because his family didn't have enough money to pay the school fees.

They lived on a small farm in the village of Masitala in Malawi. There was a terrible drought and the people in his village were struggling to survive. William wanted to help them and although he couldn't go to school, he went to his local library and found a book about windmills. The book was in English and William couldn't read English, but he studied the diagrams and the pictures and began to build his own version of a windmill. He used old bicycle parts, pieces of rubbish and even parts of a tree to make the windmill. The other people in the village thought that William was wasting his time, but they soon changed their minds when they saw that his windmill was able to provide enough energy to power four lightbulbs in his house. In fact, they began to visit William's farm in order to charge their mobile phones from his windmill.

Since then, William has made his first windmill bigger and stronger, and he's also built another windmill, which brings water into his farm's fields. He's put a solar-powered pump and water tanks into the village so that, for the first time, the people in his village have water that is safe to drink.

Visitors from all around Malawi came to look at William's project and soon there were articles about him in the local newspapers and then online. People gave money so that he could go back to school and continue his education. His dream is to bring electricity to all the people in Malawi. 'I want to help my country,' he says. 'There's lots of work to be done.'

2 Read the text and decide if each sentence is correct or incorrect.

1 William is successful now, but he wasn't when he was in his twenties.
2 He left school in 2001 because his family was very poor.
3 He borrowed a book about windmills from his school.
4 He followed the words and instructions in the book and learnt how to build a windmill.
5 He used expensive materials to make his windmill.
6 At first the people in William's village didn't think that he would succeed.
7 William's first windmill became popular with the local people because they could use it to charge their mobile phones.
8 The solar-powered pump supplies water to the village's fields.
9 Lots of people wanted to buy William's windmills.
10 William wants to help the people of Malawi.

PET Listening Part 1

In Part 1 of the Listening Paper, you have to listen to seven very short dialogues or monologues. Then you tick the correct picture for each dialogue from a choice of three.

Tip

You will be able to listen to the dialogues twice, so listen for the general meaning the first time and choose your answer. Then, when you hear the dialogues again, check your answers, concentrating on the detail.

3 Look at the pictures and the questions below. Think about what information you will listen for and match the information a–e with the questions.

   a prepositions of place
   b names of objects
   c numbers and places
   d personal descriptions and clothes
   e times

4 **[2.30]** Listen and choose the correct picture (A, B or C) for each question.

   1 What can the students take into the classroom?

   2 When will John be at the party?

   3 Who is Liz?

   4 Where is the boy's dictionary?

   5 Jenny wants to take the train to Portsmouth. Which platform should she go to?

PET Writing Part 3 (Letter)

In Part 3 of the Writing Paper, you have two options. You can write an informal letter or a story. For the letter, you read part of a letter from a friend and write a reply, answering questions from your friend.

Tip

Use different paragraphs for each new point in your letter. Always check your writing carefully for grammar, spelling and punctuation.

5 Read the task and a student's answer below. The student's answer is good, but he has made some errors. Find and correct: two spelling mistakes, two punctuation mistakes, one grammar mistake, two incorrect prepositions.

   • This is part of a letter from your friend.

In your next letter, please tell me about what you usually do at the weekend. Do you go out with friends? Do you have to do a lot of chores at home? What's your favourite activity at the weekend?

   • Now write a letter (about 100 words), answering your friend's questions.

> Hi Ana
>
> Thank you for your letter.
>
> I want to tell you about my typical weekend. I usually get over late and then I make a big brekfast for my whole family. after that I have to do some chores. I tidy my room and I sometimes take the rubbish out. I dont usually go out with friends on Saturday. I'm staying at home and I do my homework. But at Sunday, I meet up with friends and we go to the shopping centre, or we watch a DVD together. Today I'm playing Super Mario on my games console. That's my favrite activity!
>
> Best wishes
>
> Henrik

6 Read this task and write your answer.

   • This is part of a letter from your friend.

In your next letter, please tell me about your favourite book. What is it about and why do you like it? Do you read a lot?

   • Now write a letter (about 100 words), answering your friend's questions.

Writing Bank

You can find more help with writing a letter in the **Writing Bank** on page 106.

Songs

Module 1, Lesson 2

Activity

[1.06] Listen and complete the song with the present continuous form of these verbs.

go   go   take   feel   ~~wave~~   sing   sing   attract

[1.06] Then listen again and check your answers.

It's a beautiful day

Today is a new day
I *'m waving* goodbye to yesterday
I'm summoning all the good vibes my way
I'm basking in the warmth of the sun rays today

CHORUS
La La La it's a beautiful day
Things ¹_____ my way
Nothing's gonna bring me down
La La La it's a beautiful day
And I ²_____ away
Cos it's a beautiful day

The wind is in my face
I feel so alive being in this place
Surrounded by a positive embrace
I ³_____ this ride at my own pace today

CHORUS
La La La it's a beautiful day
Things ⁴_____ my way
Nothing's gonna bring me down
La La La it's a beautiful day
And I ⁵_____ away
Cos it's a beautiful day

(Repeat chorus)

It's a beautiful day
I ⁶_____ all the things I want
Things are going my way
I ⁷_____ all my power in the now
It's a beautiful day
I'm connected to the source of life
Things are going my way

(Repeat chorus)

Module 2, Lesson 6

Activity

Complete the song with the correct form of the verb in brackets.

▌1.18 ▐ Then listen and check your answers.

Shine

Put your ear to the ground
Can you hear the sound
Of a million feet marching to
The rhythm of the drum
But I hear a different voice inside
Telling me to stand my ground
I've never been one to stand in line
And wait for my turn so I

Do better than I've ever _____ (do)
Do better than I've ever _____ (do)
Do better than I've ever _____ (do)

Shine
Feel better than I've ever _____ (do)
Feel better than I've ever _____ (do)
Feel better than I've ever _____ (do)

I'm gonna shine brighter than I've ever _____
(show)
I'm gonna play harder than I've ever _____ (know)
I'm gonna sing louder than I've ever _____ (sing)
I'm gonna do better than I've ever _____ (do)
I'm gonna shine

Put your ear to the ground
Can you hear the sound
Of a million feet marching to
The rhythm of the drum
But I hear a different voice inside
Telling me to stand my ground
I've never been one to stand in line
And wait for my turn so I'm gonna

Shine
Feel better than I've ever _____ (do)
Feel better than I've ever _____ (do)
Feel better than I've ever _____ (do)

I'm gonna shine brighter than I've ever _____
(show)
I'm gonna play harder than I've ever _____ (know)
I'm gonna sing louder than I've ever _____ (sing)
I'm gonna do better than I've ever _____ (do)
I'm gonna …

Look at all the people
Looking back at me
Looking at my heroes
I just can't let it be

Shine

(Repeat chorus)

Module 5, Lesson 18

Activity

Find words in the song to match these definitions.

1 *splashing* making a noise like water or liquid
              hitting something
2 _____ lose your balance, start to fall
3 _____ hold onto something very tightly
4 _____ firm
5 _____ small pieces of bright light

▌2.15 ▐ Now listen to the song.

Keep on

Tell me something does it feel like rain
splashing down upon your face
I'll keep a moving until the end
yeah we'd probably be better off friends …

You can't hide, you can't hide it on the inside
No it wouldn't be the same
take these sparks flying all around my head

Now I won't let you slip
No, I won't let you slip and fall away
I'll keep a steady grip
'Cause I won't let you slip and fall away

Tell me what does it feel like
when you're out on that street
don't it feel like it's right in your hands
but you can't get the beat

No, I won't let you slip
No, I won't let you slip and fall away
I'll keep a steady grip
'cause I won't let you slip
and fall

Keep on, keep on

What does it feel like?
how does it feel, life, to be on your own
you're going to make it baby
no need to say you're sorry
when you're all alone now

I won't let you slip
no, I won't let you slip and fall away
I'll keep a steady grip
'cause I won't let you slip and fall away
now, I'm not going to let you fall
no, I won't let you slip
no, I won't let you slip
and fall

Keep on, keep on

Communication activities

Module 1, Lesson 3

Activity 6, Speaking and reading
Student A

Ask Student B these questions and make a note of the answers. Then use the information below to answer B's questions.

1   Where did the children go when they got to the village?
2   How many children were there?
3   Who came into the hall?
4   Where did Percy stay?
5   Had Percy ever seen chickens or pigs before?

I didn't see my parents again for three months. Then they visited me in the village. After that, they came to see me about once a month. I was always very happy to see them, but I loved living on the farm. Before I left home, I had never been out of London before, but I soon decided that I wanted to live in the countryside forever. I stayed in Hendly, with the Pritchards, for six years, until 1945, the end of the war.

Module 2, Lesson 6

Activity 6b, Speaking
Student A

You play tennis. Student B is going to ask you some questions. You can use this information to answer, but you can also make up your own answers.

1   tennis
2   for six years
3   exciting
4   being in competitions
5   training five days a week
6   fractured my ankle
7   to play at Wimbledon

Module 5, Lesson 19

Activity 5b, Speaking
Student A

Look at the information below about Advertisement A for two minutes. Then turn back to page 63 and tell Student B about the advertisement.

Advertisement A shows a picture of Salvador Dali – a famous surrealist artist. Dali had a very unusual moustache. In this advertisement the zip from a pair of Levi jeans is used instead of Dali's moustache. Salvador Dali was a genius, but his art was sometimes shocking and strange. The advertisement makes us think that Levis are fun, unusual and modern.

Module 2 Lesson 8

Activity 3, Speaking
Student A

Tell Student B about your picture. Use these words.

| score goal | jump up | triumphant | goalkeeper |
| in despair | other team | score | |

Module 3, Lesson 11

Activity 5a, Speaking and writing
Student A

Camel
Size: 1.85 m tall
Weight: 500 kg
Habitat: desert

The camel can store fat in its hump so it can survive during a drought.

Module 4, Lesson 15

Activity 6a, Speaking
Student A

Choose **one** of these two things to complain about:

1   a pair of shoes
2   a mobile phone

Prepare your complaint using the ideas below.

> 1   Pair of shoes: the heels have fallen off / they are too tight / they're both for the left foot
> 2   Mobile phone: it's already run out of battery / it won't switch on / it's not working

Don't tell your classmate your ideas.

Then turn back to page 49 and work with your classmate.

Module 6, Lesson 24

The Contradiction Game
Player A

'Serve' these statements to Player B. Listen to the replies and make sure they are the same as the short answers in the brackets. Correct Player B's mistakes. Keep the score: 1 point for every correct reply.

1   It's raining. (No, it isn't.)
2   I haven't got any money. (Yes, you have.)
3   I'm older than you. (No, you aren't.)
4   I'm not good at sport. (Yes, you are.)
5   You look tired. (No, I don't.)
6   I've known you for three years. (No, you haven't.)
7   You didn't speak to me yesterday. (Yes, I did.)
8   I saw you in town at the weekend. (No, you didn't.)
9   You can't swim faster than me. (Yes, I can.)
10 You should study more. (No, I shouldn't.)

Module 5, Lesson 17

Exercise 5, Speaking

Student A Use these expressions of quantity to describe one of the pictures to Student B.

> There is/are lots of …   There aren't many …
> There isn't much …   There are a couple of …
> There's a little …   There are a few …

Student B Listen to Student A's description. Can you guess which picture he/she is describing?

Now change roles.

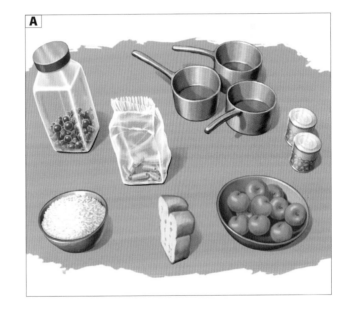

A

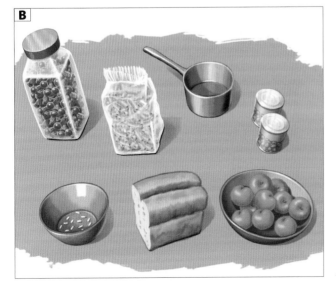

B

C

Module 1, Lesson 3

Activity 6, Speaking and reading
Student B

Use this information to answer Student A's questions. Then ask Student A the questions below and make a note of the answers.

When we arrived at Hendly Village, in Shropshire, we all went to the church hall. There were about fifty of us, I think. The people from the village came into the hall and each family took one or two children. I went to stay on a farm with the Pritchards. I'd never been to a farm before, and I'd never seen real chickens or pigs, so it was very strange at first.

1 When did Percy see his parents again?
2 How often did they visit him?
3 Did Percy enjoy staying on the farm?
4 Had Percy ever been away from London before?
5 When did Percy leave the village?

Module 2, Lesson 6

Activity 6b, Speaking
Student B

You are a swimmer. Student A is going to ask you some questions. You can use this information to answer, but you can also make up your own answers.

1 swimming
2 since I was six
3 gives you a feeling of freedom
4 winning a race
5 losing a race
6 haven't had any bad injuries
7 to swim in the Olympic Games

Module 5, Lesson 19

Activity 5a, Speaking

Module 2, Lesson 8

Activity 3, Speaking
Student B

Tell Student A about your picture. Use these words.

paralympic athletes   wheelchairs
bunches   flowers   celebrate   victory

Module 3, Lesson 11

Activity 5a, Speaking and writing
Student B

Polar bear
Size: 1.5 m tall
Weight: 340–600 kg
Habitat: the Arctic

The polar bear has very thick fur because it's very cold in the Arctic.

Module 4, Lesson 15

Activity 6a, Speaking
Student B

Choose **one** of these two things to complain about:

1   a bar of chocolate
2   a novel

Prepare your complaint using the ideas below.

> 1   A bar of chocolate: it's past its sell-by-date / it's not sweet enough / it's too sweet
> 2   A novel: I didn't like the end / there are some missing pages / I've read it before

Don't tell your classmate your ideas.

Then turn back to page 49 and work with your classmate

Module 5, Lesson 19

Exercise 5b, Speaking
Student B

Look at the information below about Advertisement B for two minutes. Then turn back to page 63 and tell Student A about the advertisement.

Advertisement B shows a picture of a beautiful animal – a stag. But the stag's antlers have been changed so that they now have bicycle handlebars on them. When we see the picture we think of something beautiful but also quite dangerous. We think of the stag running fast and also fighting. The tagline is 'Play more' and it makes us think about dangerous, unusual games. The advertisement is for a games console.

Module 6, Lesson 24

The Contradiction Game
Player B

'Serve' these statements to Player A. Listen to the replies and make sure they are the same as the short answers in the brackets. Correct Player A's mistakes. Keep the score: 1 point for every correct reply.

1   It's really cold today. (No, it isn't.)
2   I haven't got any friends. (Yes, you have.)
3   You're angry with me. (No, I'm not.)
4   You don't like watching TV. (Yes, I do.)
5   You were looking very happy when I saw you yesterday. (No, I wasn't.)
6   I haven't had anything to eat since yesterday. (Yes, you have.)
7   I don't want to go out this weekend. (Yes, you do.)
8   You shouldn't talk to Mike. (Yes, I should.)
9   You can't lend me your bike. (Yes, I can.)
10 You looked at me angrily yesterday. (No, I didn't.)

Extra material

Module 2, Lesson 6

Activity 6a, Speaking

The sports interview

1 Favourite sport? ....
2 How long? ....
3 Why do you like it? ....
4 Best thing about it? ....
5 Worst thing about it? ....
6 Worst injury? ....
7 Biggest ambition? ....

Module 4, Lesson 16

Mystery phone call

Solution

The man who answers the phone lives in the flat next door to William. His bedroom is next to William's bedroom and the walls are very thin. This man has a very loud snore and every night William has to phone him to wake him up. He then has sufficient time to go to sleep before the man starts snoring again.

Module 4, Lesson 14

Activity 1b, Presentation

Match the pictures to the names of sealife in the text.

Module 3, Lesson 12

Activity 4, Speaking

Module 4, Lesson 13

Activity 1b, Presentation

Conclusions

1   The Mary Celeste was abandoned on 25th November, 1872.
    – The last entry in the ship's logbook was written on 25th November, 1872.
2   Everyone on board had left the ship in the lifeboat and in a great hurry.
    – The lifeboat was missing and some of its navigation equipment, but the clothes and possessions
of the family and the crew were still on board.
3   The weather conditions were bad, but not bad enough to make the ship unseaworthy.
    – The sails were slightly damaged and there was some water on the decks, but the ship was seaworthy.
4   Pirates had not attacked the ship.
    – All the ship's valuable cargo was still in the hold, so pirates hadn't stolen it. If there had been pirates,
      they would have stolen the cargo.

Module 4, Lesson 15

Activity 1c, Presentation

Find out how the story on page 48 ends.

What kind of TV
programme is
Caught On Camera?

Have you ever seen
a programme like
this?

Grammar summary

1 Present tenses

1.1 Present simple

- We use the present simple to talk about repeated actions or habits.

Do you *play* football every Saturday?

Yes, I do.

Most students **do** their homework at school.

We **don't** often **go** out on Mondays.

- We also use the present simple to talk about situations that continue for a long time.

I **live** in London.

- We also use the present simple to talk about general truths.

Vegetarians **don't eat** meat.

1.2 Present continuous

- We use the present continuous to talk about what is happening now, at the moment of speaking.

Where's Billy?

He**'s playing** football.

Are you **doing** anything at the moment?   No, I'm not.

I**'m not going** anywhere.

- We also use the present continuous to talk about something that is a temporary situation.

My best friend is on holiday at the moment.
He**'s staying** with his cousins in the mountains.

- We also use the present continuous to talk about things we have planned or arranged to do in the future.

I**'m seeing** Mike at the weekend.
She**'s flying** to the US next week.

1.3 Verbs not used in the continuous Some verbs are not normally used in the continuous form, e.g. *like, hate, love, want, think, believe, know, remember, understand, imagine, see, hear, feel.*

I **don't like** cheese.

Do you **want** to go out?   Yes, I do.

I **think** I know you.

Check your grammar

Choose the correct words.

A Are you in the United Kingdom on holiday?
B Yes, I am.
A Where [1] *do you stay/are you staying* in the UK?
B [2] *I stay/I'm staying* with friends in Brighton.
A And where [3] *do you come/are you coming* from?
B I'm from Russia. [4] *I live/I'm living* in St Petersburg.
A [5] *Do you travel/Are you travelling* on your own?
B No, with my mother.
A And where is she?
B [6] *She stands/She's standing* in the queue over there. Look. [7] *She waves/She's waving* at us.
A Are you a student?
B No, [8] *I work/I'm working* for a travel company.

2 Past tenses and *used to*

2.1 Past simple We use the past simple to talk about actions and situations in the past.

My parents **packed** a suitcase and **put** a label on my coat pocket.

Did you **play** football last weekend? Yes, I did.

We **didn't go** out last night.

2.2 Past continuous We use the past continuous to talk about something that was in progress at a past time.

We **were singing** songs and we **were trying** to imagine our new homes.

Were you **playing** video games when I phoned you? Yes, I was.

I **wasn't going** home when you saw me yesterday. I **was going** out.

2.3 Past perfect We use the past perfect to talk about something that happened before the past time we are thinking about.

When I was five, in 1939, the Second World War **had** just **started**.

I **hadn't played** that video game before.

Had they already **gone** out by the time you arrived? No, they hadn't.

2.4 Used to We use *used to* to talk about past habits or situations that are finished now.

We **used to take** our gas masks everywhere!

I **didn't use to play** football, but I play it a lot now.

Did you **use to go** to that café? Yes, I did.

Check your grammar

Match the sentences to the pictures.

1 **past simple:** The bus **left** at 9.00 pm last night.
2 **past continuous:** The bus **was leaving** when I arrived.
3 **past perfect:** The bus **had left** when I arrived.
4 **used to:** The bus **used to leave** at 10.00 pm. Now it leaves at 9.00 pm.

Check your grammar

Choose the correct word to complete the sentences.

1 I arrived at school at 8.55 and my first lesson ___ at 9.00.
   a started   **b** had started
   c was starting   **d** used to start
2 I had breakfast after I ___ a shower.
   a had   **b** was having
   c had had   **d** used to have
3 She ___ when she heard the bad news.
   a was crying   **b** used to cry
   c had cried   **d** cried
4 The train suddenly stopped while it ___ the station.
   a was leaving   **b** had left
   c left   **d** used to leave
5 I didn't go out because it ___.
   a rained   **b** had rained
   c was raining   **d** used to rain
6 I eat a lot of vegetables. I didn't ___ them, but now I like them a lot.
   a liked   **b** use to like
   c wasn't liking   **d** had liked
7 I ___ my leg when I was skiing.
   a used to break   **b** had broken
   c broke   **d** was breaking
8 When I was a child I ___ up very early in the morning.
   a woke   **b** used to wake
   c had woken   **d** was waking

3 Present perfect and past simple

3.1 Present perfect We use the present perfect to talk about an indefinite time that is still not finished (e.g. sometime this week, this year, in your life).

I've been at this school for five years.

You look worried. **Have** you **lost** something? Yes, I**'ve lost** my purse.

I**'ve** never **flown** on a plane.

3.2 Past simple We use the past simple to talk about a definite time in the past (e.g. last week, two years ago, yesterday).

I **lost** my purse yesterday.

I **flew** to Spain last summer.

Check your grammar

Choose the correct words.

1 **A** Are you hungry?
   B Yes, I am. I *haven't eaten/didn't eat* anything today.
2 **A** You look tired.
   B I am tired. I *have gone/went* to bed very late last night.
3 **A** You look happy.
   B I am. I *have lost/lost* my purse this morning, but *I've found/I found* it again.
4 **A** I *have eaten/ate* Japanese food last weekend. *Have you ever eaten/Did you eat* Japanese food?
   B No, I *haven't/didn't*. *Has it been/Was it* good?
5 **A** How long *have you known/did you know* your best friend?
   B *I've known/I knew* her for two years.
6 **A** I like your new phone. How much *has it cost/did it cost*?
   B I don't know. It *has been/was* a present. My parents *have given/gave* it to me.

4 Present perfect with *just, already, yet, for, since*

- We use **just** for things which have happened recently. *Just* normally goes after the auxiliary verb *have*.

The bus **has just arrived**.

I'm tired. I**'ve just woken** up.

- We use **already** when something happened sooner than we expected. *Already* normally goes after the auxiliary verb *have*.

Where's Joe?   He**'s already left**.

Aren't you hungry?   No, I**'ve already eaten**.

- We use **yet** for something we expect to happen. *Yet* normally goes at the end of questions and negative sentences.

It's ten o'clock. **Has** Sam **woken** up **yet**?

They look new.   Yes, I **haven't worn** them **yet**.

- We use **for** with periods of time, e.g. *six years, 20 minutes, a long time*.

I**'ve been** here **for** twenty minutes.

Have you **lived** here **for** a long time?

- We use **since** for points in time, e.g. *yesterday, six o'clock, 2009*.

I**'ve been** here **since** 3.00 o'clock.

Have you **lived** here **since** September?

Check your grammar

Put the words in order to make sentences.

1 the exam/started/yet/has?
2 for/hasn't/rained/it/two months
3 have/this book/you/already/read?
4 has/I'm sorry,/the bus/just/left
5 Saturday/haven't/since/my best friend/seen/I

Check your grammar

Complete the sentences with *just, already, yet, for* or *since*.

1 **A** Let's have lunch soon.
   B Yes, we haven't seen each other ___ a really long time.
2 **A** Why don't you want to look at the photos?
   B Because I've ___ seen them three times.
3 **A** I'm sorry I'm late.
   B Don't worry. The party has only ___ started.
4 **A** Have you always lived here?
   B No, I've lived here ___ I was eleven.
5 **A** How did you do in the test?
   B I don't know. I haven't had the results ___.

5 *Must, have to, can, should, be allowed to* for obligation, permission and advice

5.1 *Must, mustn't, have to, don't have to* (obligation and necessity)

- We normally use **must** when the authority comes from the speaker.

> I **must** do my homework.

- We normally use **have to** when the authority comes from outside the speaker.

I **have to** do my homework. (The teacher says so.)

- We use **mustn't** to tell people not to do things, or when it's prohibited to do something.

You **mustn't** get up today. (My mother says …)

- We use **don't have to** when it is not necessary to do something.

I **don't have to** get up early today. (It is not necessary – it's the weekend.)

5.2 *Can* or *are allowed to* (permission)

- We use **can** or **are allowed to** when we give permission to do something.

You **can/are allowed to** eat and drink during the race.

- We use **can't** or **are not allowed to** when we say something is not permitted.

You **can't/aren't allowed to** hold the ball under the water.

5.3 *Should* or *shouldn't* (advice)

- We use **should** to give advice and say what is right and good.

The sleeves of your jacket and your trousers **should** be loose.

- We use **shouldn't** to give advice and say what is not right and good.

You **shouldn't** wear white clothing.

Check your grammar

Choose the best word to complete the sentences.

1 You ____ sit in this seat if you like.
   a must   **b** can
   c shouldn't

2 I'm sorry but you ____ go in that room. It's private.
   a don't have to   **b** should
   c aren't allowed to

3 You ____ have a licence to drive a car.
   a have to   **b** can't
   c should

4 It's late. I ____ go to bed …
   a can   **b** shouldn't
   c should

5 … because I ____ get up early in the morning.
   a shouldn't   **b** have to
   c must

6 I'm lucky. I ____ get up early tomorrow.
   a can't   **b** mustn't
   c don't have to

7 You ____ eat so quickly. You'll get stomach ache.
   a shouldn't   **b** aren't allowed to
   c mustn't

8 You ____ use your mobile in an exam.
   a must   **b** mustn't
   c should

9 We ____ wear any clothes we like at our school.
   a should   **b** don't have to
   c are allowed to

6 First and second conditional

6.1 First conditional We use the first conditional to talk about possible present or future situations.

If you **win**, you **will get** the opportunity to make your presentation at the festival.

If we **don't run**, we'll **miss** the bus.

If they **don't pass** the exam, what **will they do**?

Notice the form:

if clause	main clause
if + present simple	*will* **future**
If we **don't run**,	we'll **miss the bus.**

We use a comma after the *if* clause.

We can also start the sentence with the main clause, but notice that we don't use a comma.

We'll **miss** the bus if we **don't run**.

We can also use the word *unless* (= if not) instead of *if*.

Unless we **run**, we'll **miss** the bus.

6.2 Second conditional We use the second conditional to talk about unreal present or future situations.

If we **recycled** all the aluminium cans in the UK, we **would have** 14 million fewer full dustbins every year.

If I **didn't feel** so tired, I **would go** out.

If you **were** more polite, more people **would like** you.

Notice the form:

if clause	main clause
if + past simple	would + infinitive
If I **didn't feel** so tired,	I **would go** out.

We use a comma after the *if* clause.

We can also start the sentence with the main clause, but notice that we don't use a comma.

I **would go** out if I **didn't feel** so tired.

Check your grammar

Choose the correct form.

1 I'll give you a lift to school if it *doesn't stop/didn't stop* raining.
2 If I had a lot of money, *I'll buy/I'd buy* a laptop.
3 We *would/will* play for Manchester United if we were professional footballers.
4 Will you study English if you *go/went* to university?
5 If I eat any more chocolate, *I'll/I would* be sick.
6 *Would/Will* you have the same friends if you were famous?
7 Someone will steal your bike if you *leave/left* it there.
8 If I *see/saw* any of your friends, I'll tell you.

7 Past and present passive

- Compare these active and passive sentences.

subject	active verb	object
The Mary Celeste	**left**	New York.
The coffee	**sinks**	through the coins.

object	passive verb
The ship	**was found** by the Dei Gratia.
The bottom of the cup	**is cut off**.

- Notice the form.

Present passive

am/are/is + past participle

The bottom of the cup **is cut** off.

The two pieces of the cup **are put** back together.

Past passive

was/were + past participle

The Mary Celeste **was abandoned** on 25 November.

The ship's sails **were** slightly **damaged**.

- We use the passive:

– when it isn't important or we aren't interested in who or what does something.

It **is made** of chocolate.

– when we don't know who or what does something.

My car **was stolen** last night.

– when we don't want to say who or what does something.

I'm afraid the window **was broken**.

- We can use *by* + agent with the passive when it is important to say who or what is responsible for something.

The Mary Celeste was found **by another merchant ship, the Dei Gratia**.

This door is locked every night **by my parents**.

The man was arrested **by the police**.

Check your grammar

Complete the sentences with the correct form of the verbs in brackets. Use the present or past active or passive form.

1 The castle is very old. Do you know when it _____? (build)
2 My parents _____ our house before I was born. (build)
3 I _____ some English every day. (speak)
4 English _____ in many countries in the world. (speak)
5 My mobile _____ in the street. (find)
6 A neighbour _____ my mobile phone. (find)
7 This box _____ for recycling paper. (use)
8 I _____ these scissors for cutting hair. (use)

Check your grammar

Make passive sentences.

1 *These cars were made in India.*

1 Somebody made these cars in India.
These cars ____
2 Someone took my pen yesterday.
My pen ____
3 Someone cleans the classroom every evening.
The classroom ____
4 Someone told me the answers to the exam.
I ____

8 Adjectives

8.1 Position of adjectives

Adjectives can come in two places in a sentence:

– in front of a **noun**

Here you can explore the **breathtakingly beautiful Great Barrier Reef**.

This is a very **beautiful painting**.

I need to buy a **new phone**.

– after the verb **to be** and a few other verbs such as *look, feel, taste, smell*.

Scuba diving in Queensland Australia **is amazing**.

These shoes **are new**.

You **look angry**.

8.2 Order of adjectives

• When we use more than one adjective together, we normally put 'opinion' adjectives (*picturesque, magnificent*, etc) before 'fact' adjectives (*tropical, gigantic*, etc).

picturesque tropical islands

magnificent gigantic humpback whales

interesting new film

• When we use more than one 'fact' adjective before a noun, they normally go in this order.

size + age + shape + colour + origin + material + purpose + noun

a **large, 26-year-old, grey** elephant

a **little rope** ladder

the **metal safety** bar

Check your grammar

Put the words in order to make sentences.

1 very/my uncle/is/rich
2 don't/happy/you/look
3 town/a/live/small/I/in
4 best/my/they/friends/are
5 expensive/car/that/look at

Check your grammar

Complete the sentences with the adjectives in brackets. Put the adjectives in their usual order.

1 His father is a man. (interesting, tall)
2 Have you got any trainers? (leather, cheap, white)
3 They've bought a TV. (widescreen, new, Japanese)
4 Can you pass me one of those cups? (paper, small, yellow)
5 Have you met the teacher? (young, maths, new)

9 Countable and uncountable nouns: (*a*) *little*, (*a*) *few*, *much*, *many*, *some*, *any*, *a lot of*

• We use **much** and **(a) little** with **uncountable nouns**.

It is possible to cook good food even when you don't have **much money**.

A little cumin can make a boring dish taste much better.

• We use **many** and **(a) few** with plural countable nouns.

You don't have to buy **many** expensive **ingredients**.

Very **few** of my **friends** can cook as well as me.

Note that we use *much* and *many* mostly in questions and in negative sentences and that we normally use *a lot* in affirmative sentences.

• We use **some**, **any**, **a lot of (lots of)** with both countable and uncountable nouns.

There are **some e-mails** for you.

I've got **some news** for you.

There aren't **any e-mails** for you.

There isn't **any news** for you.

I get **a lot of visitors**.

I spent **a lot of time**.

Note that we generally use *some* in affirmative sentences and *any* in negative sentences. Also note that we normally use *any* in questions but that we often use *some* when we expect people to say 'yes' to our question.

Check your grammar

Choose the correct word to complete the sentences.

1   I haven't got ___ money.
    a some   **b** any
    c many   **d** a little

2   Do you like films? I've got ___ very good DVDs.
    a much   **b** some
    c many   **d** any

3   Would you like ___ more soup?
    a many   **b** a few
    c few   **d** some

4   There are ___ students in my class.
    a little   **b** much
    c lots of **d** many

5   How ___ time have you got?
    a a lot of **b** any
    c much   **d** many

6   I haven't got ___ friends.
    a many   **b** much
    c few   **d** some

7   I've got ___ jobs to do today.
    a little   **b** a lot of
    c much   **d** many

8   Only ___ students passed the test.
    a a few   **b** many
    c a lot of **d** a little

9   You only need to put ___ salt in the soup.
    a much   **b** many
    c a little **d** few

10   Modals: speculation and deduction: *could, may/might, can't* and *must*

- We use **could** and **might** to say something is possible.

What's that bright light in the sky?

*I don't know. It **could be** a satellite.*

It **could be** an advertisement for a film or it **might be** an advertisement for a city.

I'm not sure what I'm going to do. I **might go** out.

- We use **must** in deductions to say we are sure about something.

*You **must be** cold.*

His foot **must hurt**.

You **must know** Dave. He lives in the same street as you.

- We use **can't** (not *mustn't*) as the negative of *must* to say something is impossible.

*You **can't be** tired. You've just woken up.*

I'm tired.

This **can't be** an advertisement for a beauty product.

Notice that we use *could/might/can/must* with the infinitive without *to*.

Check your grammar

Rewrite the sentences. Use the modal verbs in brackets.

Perhaps I will go to the cinema tonight. (might)

I might go to the cinema tonight.

1   Perhaps I will pass the test. (might)
2   Perhaps they are hungry. (could)
3   Perhaps I'll miss the bus. (might)
4   Perhaps I'll see you tomorrow. (could)

Check your grammar

Answer the questions. Use *must* or *can't* and the reasons in brackets.

Is she worried? (She's lost her mobile phone.)

She must be worried. She's lost her mobile phone.

1 Will they win? (The other team isn't very good.)
2 Is he ill? (He's going out with his friends tonight.)
3 Are they English? (They are speaking with an American accent.)
4 Is it late? (All the shops are closed.)
5 Is she a doctor? (She's too young.)
6 Does he know where to go? (He's lived here all his life.)

11 Direct speech / Reported speech

11.1 Direct speech

In direct speech we use the exact words the other person says and we use quotation marks ('…') or ("…").

Mel said, 'I **know** your sister.'

Craig asked Mel, 'Where **did** you **get** them?'

11.2 Reported speech

In reported speech we change some of the words the other person uses and we do not use quotation marks. Also, we do not use question marks in reported speech.

Mel **said** she **knew** Craig's sister.

Craig **asked** Mel where she **had got** them.

Notice that when we use a past reporting verb (e.g. *said*, *told*, *asked*) the tense in reported speech normally changes. When we use a present reporting verb the tense doesn't change.

Mel **says** she **knows** Craig's sister.

If the situation is still true or a known fact, we can also keep the original tense.

She **said** the café **is** open on Sundays.

Direct speech	Reported speech
'I **know** your sister.'	Mel **said** she **knew** Craig's sister.
'I **like** your sunglasses.'	Craig **told** Mel he **liked** her sunglasses.
'Where **did** you get them?'	Craig **asked** Mel where she **had got** them.
'**Are** you into music?'	Craig **asked** if Mel **was** into music.
'**Can** you **pass** me my bag?'	Mel **asked** Craig **to pass** him her bag.
'**Look** us **up** on Facebook.'	Mel **told** Craig **to look** them **up** on Facebook.
'**Don't forget** your books.'	Craig **told** Mel **not to forget** her books.

Notice that when there is no question word in direct speech (e.g. *where, when, what*) we use *if* to introduce the reported question.

We often use *that* in reported speech affirmative and negative sentences.

Mel **said that** she **knew** Craig's sister.

Check your grammar

Choose the correct word to complete the sentences.

1 He ___ he couldn't go out.
  a says   b said
  c told   d asked
2 I asked my friend where he ___ in such a hurry.
  a goes   b is going
  c was going   d went
3 The teacher told us ___ late.
  a wasn't   b not be
  c not being   d not to be
4 She told us she ___ to our teacher.
  a had spoken   b to speak
  c speaking   d speak
5 I asked them ___ they liked football.
  a what   b who
  c if   d do
6 She asked me ___ my name was.
  a who   b what
  c if   d when
7 I told him that I ___ my homework.
  a had finished   b finish
  c has finish   d finished
8 I asked them what they ___ when I saw them yesterday.
  a did want   b do want
  c want   d wanted

12 Tag questions

- **Form** A question tag is an expression like *isn't it?*
  do they? at the end of a statement.

We form question tags with an auxiliary verb (e.g. *be,*
have, can) and a personal pronoun (e.g. *it, they, she*).
We use the same auxiliary verb in the tag as in the
statement.

We normally use a negative tag with affirmative
statements and a positive tag with a negative
statement.

Affirmative statement	Negative tag
+	−
You **are** American,	**aren't** you?
Your name **is** Lance,	**isn't** it?
It **is** really cool,	**isn't** it?

Negative statement	Affirmative tag
−	+
We **haven't** met before,	**have** we?
It **wasn't** my accent,	**was** it?
You **aren't** kidding me,	**are** you?

Notice that we use short answers to answer tag
questions.

You aren't a vegetarian, are you?
Yes, I am./No, I'm not.

- **Use** We often use tag questions to check if
  something is true or to ask someone to agree with
  us. When we do this we use a falling intonation
  (the voice goes down).

It is really cool, isn't it?

When we use a tag question to ask a real question
(when we are not sure of the answer), we use a rising
intonation (the voice goes up).

We haven't met before, have we?

Check your grammar

Add a question tag to these statements.

1   You're tired.
2   She wasn't sleeping.
3   It is raining.
4   There isn't any food.
5   He had an accident.
6   You haven't got any money.

Irregular verbs

Present simple	Past simple	Past participle	Present simple	Past simple	Past participle
be	was/were	been	learn	learnt	learnt
become	became	become	leave	left	left
begin	began	begun	lose	lost	lost
blow	blew	blown	make	made	made
break	broke	broken	meet	met	met
bring	brought	brought	put on	put on	put on
build	built	built	read	read	read
buy	bought	bought	ride	rode	ridden
choose	chose	chosen	run	ran	ran
cut	cut	cut	say	said	said
do	did	done	see	saw	seen
drink	drank	drunk	send	sent	sent
drive	drove	driven	shoot	shot	shot
eat	ate	eaten	sit	sat	sat
fall	fell	fallen	sleep	slept	slept
feed	fed	fed	speak	spoke	spoken
find	found	found	spend	spent	spent
fly	flew	flown	swim	swam	swum
forget	forgot	forgotten	take	took	taken
get	got	got	think	thought	thought
go	went	gone	throw	threw	thrown
hang out	hung out	hung out	understand	understood	understood
have	had	had	wake up	woke up	woken up
hit	hit	hit	wear	wore	worn
hurt	hurt	hurt	win	won	won
keep	kept	kept	write	wrote	written

Vocabulary bank

1 Compound nouns

A compound noun is a noun made from two or more words. Usually the second part of the compound noun tells us what the thing/person is, and the first part describes or qualifies it.

One-word compound nouns

Some compound nouns are written as one word:
policeman
bookmark

Two-word compound nouns

Some compound nouns are written as two words:
fish tank
dining table

Hyphenated compound nouns

Very few compound nouns use hyphens:
T-shirt
pen-friend (*penfriend* is also acceptable)

Other examples

airport	bedroom
blackberry	chest of drawers
cupboard	driving licence
football	greenhouse
head teacher	high school
keyboard	post office
swimming pool	washing machine
whiteboard	

2 Verb phrases

The verbs *make* and *do* are very commonly used in English. There are many phrases which use these verbs and it's important to learn and remember the correct verb for each phrase.

Phrases with *make* or *do*

make	do
arrangements	homework
a phone call	the ironing
a decision	the cooking
a mistake	the dishes
a noise	a job
money	an exam
an excuse	the cleaning
a cup of tea / coffee	your hair
a mess	nothing
your bed	
a meal	

3 *get*

The verb **get** is very useful because it has lots of different meanings:

get = arrive

> I **got** to the station five minutes before the train left.
> She'll **get** to London at five o'clock this afternoon.

get = receive

> What did you **get** for your birthday?
> I **got** a new games console and a surfboard.

get = obtain

> Can you **get** me some cheese from the supermarket?
> I'll **get** your bag for you when I go back to the classroom.

get + adjective

We use *get* with lots of different adjectives and prepositions. Here are some commonly used phrases with *get*:

> get engaged / married / divorced
> get ready
> get on / off a bus / bike
> get in / out of a car

4 Opposites

Fifty opposites

above	below	hot	cold
after	before	in	out
always	never	increase	decrease
asleep	awake	inside	outside
attack	defend	intelligent	unintelligent
beautiful	ugly	kind	unkind
bitter	sweet	long	short
clean	dirty	loud	quiet
clever	stupid	low	high
dark	light	more	less
day	night	narrow	wide
dead	alive	no	yes
delicious	disgusting	nothing	everything
early	late	on	off
easy	difficult	open	closed/shut
expensive	cheap	polite	rude/impolite
false	true	pull	push
far	near/close	rich	poor
fast	slow	right	left
fat	thin	right	wrong
find	lose	small	big/large
full	empty	soft	hard
give	take	tall	short
good	bad	up	down
guilty	innocent	with	without

5 Prepositions: *at, on, in*

Time

- We use *at* for precise times.
  at 9.30
  at bedtime
  at dawn

- We also use *at* in the following time phrases.
  at night
  at the weekend
  at Christmas/Easter
  at the same time

- We use *on* for days and dates.
  on my birthday
  on 23 September
  on Christmas Eve

- We also use *on* in the following time phrases.
  on Tuesday morning
  on Saturday afternoons

- We use *in* for months, years and long periods of time.
  in April last year
  in 1994
  in the 17th century

- We also use *in* in the following time phrases.
  in the morning
  in the evenings

Place

- We use *at* for a specific point.
  at the bookshop
  at the crossroads

- We also use *at* in the following phrases.
  at home/work
  at school/university/college
  at the bottom/top

- We use *on* for a flat surface.
  on the motorway
  on the river
  on the fourth floor

- We also use *on* for the following phrases.
  on a bus/bicycle/train (but *in a taxi/car*)
  on a horse/camel
  on my way

- We use *in* for an enclosed space and for countries and towns.
  in the kitchen
  in the garden
  in a car
  in America
  in London

- We also use *in* for the following phrases.
  in hospital
  in a lift
  in the newspaper
  in Maple Street (but *on the High Street*)

6 Prefixes: *in-, il-, ir-, im-, un-, dis-, pre-, re-, sub-, super-*

We use prefixes at the beginning of words to alter their meanings.

To make the opposite of a word, we often use *in-, il-, ir-* or *im-*.

- We use *in-* before most letters.
  decent   →   **in**decent
  capable   →   **in**capable

- We use *il-* before words starting with the letter l.
  legal   →   **il**legal
- We use *ir-* before words starting with the letter r.
  regular   →   **ir**regular
- We use *im-* before words starting with the letters m or p.
  modest   →   **im**modest
  patient   →   **im**patient

- We can also use *un-* or *dis-* to make the opposite of a word.
  popular   →   **un**popular
  satisfied   →   **dis**satisfied

We use *pre-* to mean before and *re-* to mean again.

mature   →   **pre**mature
heat   →   **pre**heat
apply   →   **re**apply
pay   →   **re**pay

We use *sub-* to mean under (or smaller/worse) and *super-* to mean over or above (or bigger/better).

marine   →   **sub**marine
standard   →   **sub**standard
man   →   **super**man
market   →   **super**market

7 Suffixes: *-ful, -less, -ly, -ness*

We use suffixes at the end of words to alter their meanings.

- We use *-ful* to mean with something and *-less* to mean without something.
  hope   →   hope**ful**
                           hope**less**
  use   →   use**ful**
                           use**less**
  meaning   →   meaning**ful**
                           meaning**less**

- We use *-ly* to turn an adjective into an adverb.
  calm   →   calm**ly**
  painful   →   painful**ly**
  loud   →   loud**ly**

We use *-ness* to turn an adjective into a noun.

happy   →   happi**ness**
lonely   →   loneli**ness**
dark   →   dark**ness**

Writing bank

1 Stories

Setting the scene

> It was cold and dark.
> The sun was shining and it was a beautiful day.
> It was Saturday afternoon and the shopping centre was crowded.

Use the past simple to talk about finished actions in the past.

> He **picked** up the letter and **put it** in his pocket.
> She **ran** down the street and **hid** behind a door.

Use the past continuous to talk about continuing actions in the past.

> The children **were playing** on the beach and Mr Smith **was reading** his newspaper.
> He **was waving** at her, but she didn't see him.

Use adjectives and adverbs to add drama to your story.

> She was a **tall beautiful** woman with **long blond** hair.
> He shouted **furiously** at the boy.
> Steve looked **nervously** at his watch.

Use linking words and sequencing words to make your writing more fluent and to join sentences together.

Sequencing words

To start a story	At the beginning, …
	At first, …
	First of all, …
	There was once …
The middle of the story	Then, …
	After that …
	When she heard the noise, she ran downstairs.
	While Tim was sleeping, his dog ate his slippers
To finish the story	Finally, …
	At the end, …
	At last, …

Cause, result and purpose

(cause) *so* (result)	I was very tired, **so** I went to bed early.
(result) *because* (cause)	I went to bed early **because** I was very tired.
(action) *in order to* (purpose)	I went to bed early **in order to** get some sleep.

Contrast

although	**Although** she was very clever, she didn't enjoy school.
but	He saw her **but** he didn't speak to her.
despite	**Despite** the cold weather, she was only wearing a T-shirt and shorts.

2 Short communicative messages

Saying thank you

Thank you so much for	the lovely present.
I'm really grateful for	the very kind gift.
I'd like to thank you for	the amazing surprise.
Many thanks for	the meal.

Giving more detail

I particularly enjoyed	the wonderful music.
I loved	the food.
It was great	to see my old friends again.
I thought that	the scarf was lovely. the party was great.

Saying why

I loved your present because …	it fits me perfectly. it's just what I need. it looks wonderful. it's very warm/practical/useful/stylish.

Saying sorry

I'm so sorry that I'm afraid that It's such a shame that	I can't come to your party.
I was so sorry to hear that	you have been ill.

Inviting

Would you like to	come out for dinner play tennis	next week? tomorrow? on Saturday night?
Are you free		
I'd love to invite you to	my house dinner the cinema	next week. tomorrow. on Saturday night.

Making suggestions

Why don't we / Shall we	meet outside the post office? visit your sister?
How about / What about	playing football? taking the train to London?
Let's	go to the park.

Asking for a response/Finishing the message

Let me know what you think.
Many thanks again.
Look forward to hearing from you.

3 Informal letters

Beginning the letter

Dear (first name)
Hi (first name)

First sentence

How are you?
I hope you are well.
Thank you so much for your letter.
It was lovely to hear from you.

Stating the main purpose of your letter

I want to tell you about	my typical weekend.
You asked me about	my favourite film.
This is	a traditional meal in our country.
I'll try to tell you something about	our town.
My favourite festival is	the festival of lights.

Giving more details

We usually/often/sometimes	go out for lunch.
	make amazing costumes.
	play loud music.
	eat rice and vegetables in a special sauce.
I love the film because	the acting was great.
	the plot was very strong.
	it was so romantic/exciting/scary.
It's my favourite book because	the characters are so real.
	it makes me laugh.
	it's very well written.

Saying goodbye

With best wishes
All the best
Take care and see you soon
Lots of love

Word List

Module 1, Lesson 1

airline	/ˈeə(r)ˌlaɪn/
amazing	/əˈmeɪzɪŋ/
audio engineering	/ˈɔːdiəʊ endʒɪˌnɪərɪŋ/
be crazy about something	/biː ˈkreɪzi əbaʊt ˌsʌmθɪŋ/
be fond of something	/biː ˈfɒnd əv ˌsʌmθɪŋ/
be good at something	/biː ˈɡʊd æt ˌsʌmθɪŋ/
be interested in something	/biː ˈɪntrəstɪd ɪn ˌsʌmθɪŋ/
change his/her mind	/ˈtʃeɪndʒ hɪz/ hɜː(r) ˌmaɪnd/
check something out	/ˌtʃek ˌsʌmθɪŋ ˈaʊt/
concentrate on something	/ˈkɒns(ə)nˌtreɪt ɒn ˌsʌmθɪŋ/
creative	/kriˈeɪtɪv/
determined	/dɪˈtɜː(r)mɪnd/
DJ	/ˈdiːˌdʒeɪ/
dream of something	/ˈdriːm əv ˌsʌmθɪŋ/
fashion	/ˈfæʃ(ə)n/
flat	/flæt/
girlfriend	/ˈɡɜː(r)lˌfrend/
hang out together	/ˌhæŋ ˈaʊt təˌɡeðə(r)/
jewellery	/ˈdʒuːəlri/
journalist	/ˈdʒɜː(r)nəlɪst/
language	/ˈlæŋɡwɪdʒ/
nearby	/ˌnɪə(r)ˈbaɪ/
poster	/ˈpəʊstə(r)/
pretty	/ˈprɪti/
send pictures	/ˌsend ˈpɪktʃə(r)s/
shy	/ʃaɪ/
smart	/smɑː(r)t/
sociable	/ˈsəʊʃəb(ə)l/
spend time together	/ˌspend ˈtaɪm təˌɡeðə(r)/
surf	/sɜː(r)f/
text	/tekst/
think of something	/ˈθɪŋk əv ˌsʌmθɪŋ/

Module 1, Lesson 2

announce	/əˈnaʊns/
carry out	/ˈkæri ˈaʊt/
chemistry	/ˈkemɪstri/
chop	/tʃɒp/
chores	/tʃɔː(r)/
desert	/ˈdezə(r)t/
driver's licence	/ˈdraɪvə(r)s ˌlaɪs(ə)ns/
driving lesson	/ˈdraɪvɪŋ ˌles(ə)n/
electricity	/ɪˌlekˈtrɪsəti/
experiment	/ɪkˈsperɪmənt/
fill something in	/ˌfɪl ˌsʌmθɪŋ ˈɪn/gɪg/gɪg/
indigenous language	/ɪnˈdɪdʒənəs ˌlæŋɡwɪdʒ/
light	/laɪt/
look after something/ someone	/ˌlʊk ˈɑːftə(r) ˌsʌmθɪŋ ˌsʌmwʌn/
look forward to something	/ˌlʊk ˈfɔː(r)wə(r)d tu: ˌsʌmθɪŋ/
podcast	/ˈpɒdˌkɑːst/
practise	/ˈpræktɪs/

put something off	/ˌpʊt ˌsʌmθɪŋ ˈɒf/
rehearsal	/rɪˈhɜː(r)s(ə)l/
run away	/ˌrʌn əˈweɪ/
set	/set/
stage	/steɪdʒ/
stay up	/ˌsteɪ ˈʌp/
sunlight	/ˈsʌnˌlaɪt/
venue	/ˈvenjuː/

Module 1, Lesson 3

bomb	/bɒm/
cap	/kæp/
countryside	/ˈkʌntriˌsaɪd/
cry	/kraɪ/
evacuate	/ɪˈvækjueɪt/
evacuation	/ɪˌvækjuˈeɪʃ(ə)n/
evacuee	/ɪˌvækjuˈiː/
gas mask	/ˈɡæs ˌmɑːsk/
government	/ˈɡʌvə(r)nmənt/
label	/ˈleɪb(ə)l/
move	/muːv/
pack	/pæk/
packet	/ˈpækɪt/
safe	/seɪf/
suitcase	/ˈsuːtˌkeɪs/
tie	/taɪ/
town hall	/ˌtaʊn ˈhɔːl/
travel	/ˈtræv(ə)l/
uniform	/ˈjuːnɪfɔː(r)m/

Module 1, Lesson 4

altitude	/ˈæltɪˌtjuːd/
Christmas card	/ˈkrɪsməs ˌkɑː(r)d/
Christmas pudding	/ˌkrɪsməs ˈpʊdɪŋ/
distance	/ˈdɪstəns/
drag	/dræɡ/
expedition	/ˌekspəˈdɪʃ(ə)n/
feel sick	/ˈfiːl ˌsɪk/
frozen	/ˈfrəʊz(ə)n/
harsh	/hɑː(r)ʃ/
New Year's Eve	/ˌnjuː jɪə(r)s ˈiːv/
regime	/reɪˈʒiːm/
sledge	/sledʒ/
South Pole	/ˌsaʊθ ˈpəʊl/
stamina	/ˈstæmɪnə/
temperature	/ˈtemprɪtʃə(r)/
tent	/tent/
tinsel	/ˈtɪns(ə)l/
training regime	/ˈtreɪnɪŋ reɪˌʒiːm/
trek (n)	/trek/
trek (v)	/trek/
tyre	/ˈtaɪə(r)/
victorious	/vɪkˈtɔːriəs/

Module 1, Extra Special

fist	/fɪst/
halter	/ˈhɔːltə(r)/
hand	/hænd/
jacket	/ˈdʒækɪt/
jaw	/dʒɔː/
jodhpurs	/ˈdʒɒdpə(r)z/
look like someone	/ˈlʊk laɪk ˌsʌmwʌn/
riding hat	/ˈraɪdɪŋ ˌhæt/
shin	/ʃɪn/
waist	/weɪst/

Module 2, Lesson 5

aerobics	/eəˈrəʊbɪks/
balanced diet	/ˈbælənst ˌdaɪət/
cereals	/ˈsɪəriəls/
citrus fruit	/ˈsɪtrəs ˌfruːt/
exercise	/ˈeksə(r)saɪz/
expert	/ˈekspɜː(r)t/
hang-gliding	/ˈhæŋ ˌglaɪdɪŋ/
hockey	/ˈhɒki/
hydrate	/ˈhaɪˌdreɪt/
jogging	/ˈdʒɒgɪŋ/
rock climbing	/ˈrɒk ˌklaɪmɪŋ/
roller skating	/ˈrəʊlə(r) ˌskeɪtɪŋ/
running	/ˈrʌnɪŋ/
strenuous	/ˈstrenjuəs/
ten pin bowling	/ˌtenpɪn ˈbəʊlɪŋ/
volleyball	/ˈvɒliˌbɔːl/
weight training	/ˈweɪt ˌtreɪnɪŋ/

Module 2, Lesson 6

ambition	/æmˈbɪʃ(ə)n/
bruise	/bruːz/
buzz	/bʌz/
compete	/kəmˈpiːt/
competition	/ˌkɒmpəˈtɪʃ(ə)n/
cut	/kʌt/
fracture	/ˈfræktʃə(r)/
freedom	/ˈfriːdəm/
get hurt	/ˌget ˈhɜː(r)t/
injury	/ˈɪndʒəri/
snowboarding	/ˈsnəʊˌbɔː(r)dɪŋ/
sprain	/spreɪn/
train	/treɪn/

Module 2, Lesson 7

attack	/əˈtæk/
basketball	/ˈbɑːskɪtˌbɔːl/
baton	/ˈbætɒn/
bow	/baʊ/
carry	/ˈkæri/
crash helmet	/ˈkræʃ ˌhelmɪt/
cross	/krɒs/
cycle racing	/ˌsaɪk(ə)l ˈreɪsɪŋ/

dribble	/ˈdrɪb(ə)l/
hand over	/ˌhænd ˈəʊvə(r)/
hit	/hɪt/
hold	/həʊld/
judo	/ˈdʒuːdəʊ/
kick	/kɪk/
lane	/leɪn/
lift	/lɪft/
net	/net/
opponent	/əˈpəʊnənt/
overtake	/ˌəʊvə(r)ˈteɪk/
palm	/pɑːm/
pass	/pɑːs/
punch	/pʌntʃ/
push	/pʊʃ/
relay	/rɪˈleɪ/
return	/rɪˈtɜː(r)n/
roll	/rəʊl/
serve	/sɜː(r)v/
shoulder	/ˈʃəʊldə(r)/
splash	/splæʃ/
start	/stɑː(r)t/
stay	/steɪ/
stop someone doing something	/ˈstɒp ˌsʌmwʌn ˌduːɪŋ ˌsʌmθɪŋ/
table tennis	/ˈteɪb(ə)l ˌtenɪs/
take over	/ˈteɪk ˌəʊvə(r)/
throw	/θrəʊ/
touch	/tʌtʃ/
track	/træk/
water polo	/ˈwɔːtə(r) ˌpəʊləʊ/
weigh	/weɪ/
wheel	/wiːl/

Module 2, Lesson 8

active	/ˈæktɪv/
aerobic exercise	/eəˈrəʊbɪk ˌeksə(r)saɪz/
bat	/bæt/
blood	/blʌd/
brain	/breɪn/
breathe	/briːð/
bunch of flowers	/ˈbʌntʃ əv ˌflaʊə(r)z/
cross-country skiing	/ˌkrɒskʌntri ˈskiːɪŋ/
endorphin	/enˈdɔː(r)fɪn/
flexible	/ˈfleksəb(ə)l/
heart	/hɑː(r)t/
in despair	/ˌɪn dɪˈspeə(r)/
mood	/muːd/
muscle	/ˈmʌs(ə)l/
oxygen	/ˈɒksɪdʒ(ə)n/
paralympic athlete	/pærəˌlɪmpɪk ˈæθliːt/
pump	/pʌmp/
push-up	/ˈpʊʃʌp/
quicken	/ˈkwɪkən/
rowing	/ˈrəʊɪŋ/
skateboard	/ˈskeɪtˌbɔː(r)d/
sweaty	/ˈsweti/
touch your toes	/ˌtʌtʃ jɔː(r) ˈtəʊz/
triumphant	/traɪˈʌmfənt/
wheelchair	/ˈwiːlˌtʃeə(r)/

Module 2, Extra Special

afford	/əˈfɔː(r)d/
bucket	/ˈbʌkɪt/
get fit	/ˌget ˈfɪt/
I tell you what	/aɪ ˈtel juː ˌwɒt/
join	/dʒɔɪn/
member	/ˈmembə(r)/
unfit	/ʌnˈfɪt/
vacuum	/ˈvækjʊəm/

Module 3, Lesson 9

amount to something	/əˈmaʊnt tə ˌsʌmθɪŋ/
atmosphere	/ˈætməsˌfɪə(r)/
aviator	/ˈeɪviˌeɪtə(r)/
cure	/kjʊə(r)/
elect	/ɪˈlekt/
fall out	/ˈfɔːl ˌaʊt/
get tired of	/ˌget ˈtaɪə(r)d əv/
greenhouse	/ˈgriːnˌhaʊs/
isolated	/ˈaɪsəˌleɪtɪd/
it doesn't matter	/ɪt ˈdʌz(ə)nt ˌmætə(r)/
last	/lɑːst/
prediction	/prɪˈdɪkʃ(ə)n/
prime minister	/ˌpraɪm ˈmɪnɪstə(r)/
screen	/skriːn/
technological	/ˌteknəˈlɒdʒɪk(ə)l/
underground	/ˈʌndə(r)ˌgraʊnd/

Module 3, Lesson 10

aluminium	/ˌæləˈmɪniəm/
biodegradable	/ˌbaɪəʊdɪˈgreɪdəb(ə)l/
clear up	/ˌklɪə(r) ˈʌp/
cloth	/klɒθ/
come across	/ˌkʌm əˈkrɒs/
cut down on	/ˌkʌt ˈdaʊn ɒn/
decompose	/ˌdiːkəmˈpəʊz/
donation	/dəʊˈneɪʃ(ə)n/
fine	/faɪn/
give something out	/ˈgɪv sʌmθɪŋ ˌaʊt/
litter	/ˈlɪtə(r)/
messy	/ˈmesi/
pick up	/ˌpɪk ˈʌp/
plastic	/ˈplæstɪk/
polluted	/pəˈluːtɪd/
raise money	/ˈreɪz ˌmʌni/
recycle	/riːˈsaɪk(ə)l/
throw away	/ˌθrəʊ əˈweɪ/
turn up to	/ˌtɜː(r)n ˈʌp tuː/
waterproof	/ˈwɔːtə(r)ˌpruːf/
wellies	/ˈwelis/
workshop	/ˈwɜː(r)kˌʃɒp/

Module 3, Lesson 11

adaptation	/ˌædæpˈteɪʃ(ə)n/
bill	/bɪl/
branch	/brɑːntʃ/
burrow	/ˈbʌrəʊ/
camouflage	/ˈkæməˌflɑːʒ/
drought	/draʊt/
extreme (adj)	/ɪkˈstriːm/
extreme (n)	/ɪkˈstriːm/
fur	/fɜː(r)/
habitat	/ˈhæbɪtæt/
humid	/ˈhjuːmɪd/
mate	/meɪt/
penguin	/ˈpeŋgwɪn/
poisonous	/ˈpɔɪz(ə)nəs/
prey	/preɪ/
shady	/ˈʃeɪdi/
toucan	/ˈtuːkən/
tropical	/ˈtrɒpɪk(ə)l/
tundra	/ˈtʌndrə/

Module 3, Lesson 12

age limit	/ˈeɪdʒ ˌlɪmɪt/
amateur	/ˈæmətə(r)/
astronomer	/əˈstrɒnəmə(r)/
awesome	/ˈɔːs(ə)m/
float	/fləʊt/
free of charge	/ˈfriː əv ˌtʃɑː(r)dʒ/
gravity	/ˈgrævəti/
light pollution	/ˈlaɪt pəˌluːʃ(ə)n/
medical check	/ˈmedɪk(ə)l ˌtʃek/
safety procedure	/ˈseɪfti prəˌsiːdʒə(r)/
speed of sound	/ˈspiːd əv ˌsaʊnd/
telescope	/ˈteliˌskəʊp/

Module 3, Extra Special

beg	/beg/
cloak	/kləʊk/
darkness	/ˈdɑː(r)knəs/
daylight	/ˈdeɪˌlaɪt/
disguise	/dɪsˈgaɪz/
Inuit	/ˈɪnuɪt/; /ˈɪnjuɪt/
scratch	/skrætʃ/

Module 4, Lesson 13

abandon	/ə'bændən/
absorb	/əb'zɔː(r)b/
alcohol	/'ælkə,hɒl/
board	/bɔː(r)d/
cargo	/'kɑː(r)gəʊ/
conclude	/kən'kluːd/
crew	/kruː/
deck	/dek/
drift	/drɪft/
hold	/həʊld/
inquiry	/ɪn'kwaɪəri/
lifeboat	/'laɪf,bəʊt/
logbook	/'lɒg,bʊk/
merchant ship	/'mɜː(r)tʃ(ə)nt ,ʃɪp/
navigation equipment	/,nævɪgeɪʃ(ə)n ɪ'kwɪpmənt/
officer	/'ɒfɪsə(r)/
on board	/,ɒn 'bɔː(r)d/
pirate	/'paɪrət/
pour	/pɔː(r)/
sail	/seɪl/
sailor	/'seɪlə(r)/
shake	/ʃeɪk/
sink	/sɪŋk/
tissue paper	/'tɪʃuː ,peɪpə(r)/
trick	/trɪk/
(un)seaworthy	/(ʌn)'siː,wɜː(r)ði/

Module 4, Lesson 14

break off	/,breɪk 'ɒf/
breathtaking	/'breθ,teɪkɪŋ/
bright	/braɪt/
brilliant	/'brɪljənt/
coral (adj)	/'kɒrəl/
coral (n)	/'kɒrəl/
crystal clear	/,krɪst(ə)l 'klɪə(r)/
delicate	/'delɪkət/
encounter	/ɪn'kaʊntə(r)/
gigantic	/dʒaɪ'gæntɪk/
golden	/'gəʊld(ə)n/
magnificent	/mæg'nɪfɪs(ə)nt/
massive	/'mæsɪv/
picturesque	/,pɪktʃə'resk/
polyp	/'pɒlɪp/
reef	/riːf/
scuba diving	/'skuːbə ,daɪvɪŋ/
skeleton	/'skelɪt(ə)n/
species	/'spiːʃiːz/
spectacular	/spek'tækjʊlə(r)/
sun-soaked	/'sʌn,səʊkt/

Module 4, Lesson 15

burnt	/bɜː(r)nt/
cobweb	/'kɒb,web/
concrete	/'kɒŋkriːt/
disgusting	/dɪs'gʌstɪŋ/
freezing	/'friːzɪŋ/
incredibly	/ɪn'kredəbli/
inedible	/ɪn'edəb(ə)l/
mattress	/'mætrəs/
radiator	/'reɪdi,eɪtə(r)/
spooky	/'spuːki/
unbelievably	/,ʌnbɪ'liːvəb(ə)li/

Module 4, Lesson 16

ancient	/'eɪnʃ(ə)nt/
hull	/hʌl/
irrigation	/,ɪrɪ'geɪʃ(ə)n/
landing strip	/'lændɪŋ ,strɪp/
low pressure	/,ləʊ 'preʃə(r)/
measuring rod	/'meʒərɪŋ ,rɒd/
racetrack	/'reɪs,træk/
waterspout	/'wɔːtə(r),spaʊt/

Module 5, Lesson 17

banquet	/'bæŋkwɪt/
broccoli	/'brɒkəli/
canteen	/kæn'tiːn/
carbohydrate	/,kɑː(r)bəʊ'haɪdreɪt/
pulses	/'pʌlsɪz/
spice	/spaɪs/
stew	/stjuː/
stir fry	/'stɜː(r) ,fraɪ/
three-course meal	/'θriː kɔː(r)s ,miːl/
wok	/wɒk/

Module 5, Lesson 18

borrow	/'bɒrəʊ/
hair straighteners	/'heə(r) ,streɪt(ə)n(ə)rs/
in a bad mood	/ɪn ə 'bæd ,muːd/
in a lot of trouble	/ɪn ə 'lɒt əv ,trʌb(ə)l/
in a mess	/ɪn ə 'mes/
on his way	/ɒn ,hɪz 'weɪ/
on my own	/ɒn ,maɪ 'əʊn/
on time	/ɒn 'taɪm/

Module 5, Lesson 19

advertisement	/əd'vɜ:(r)tɪsmənt/
ape	/eɪp/
brand	/brænd/
campaign	/kæm'peɪn/
consumer	/kən'sju:mə(r)/
glamorous	/'glæmərəs/
logo	/'ləʊgəʊ/
product	/'prɒdʌkt/
tagline	/'tæg ˌlaɪn/
wrinkled	/'rɪŋk(ə)ld/

Module 5, Lesson 20

atmosphere	/'ætməsˌfɪə(r)/
bargain	/'bɑ:(r)gɪn/
blend	/blend/
floral	/'flɔ:rəl/
hang out	/ˌhæŋ 'aʊt/
herbal	/'hɜ:(r)b(ə)l/
ingredients	/ɪn'gri:diənt/
lively	/'laɪvli/
organic	/ɔ:(r)'gænɪk/
pastries	/'peɪstrɪs/
pop	/pɒp/
range	/reɪndʒ/
recommend	/ˌrekə'mend/
surroundings	/sə'raʊndɪŋz/
tasty	/'teɪsti/
vegetarian	/ˌvedʒə'teəriən/

Module 5, Extra Special

necklace	/'nekləs/
unusual	/ʌn'ju:ʒʊəl/
waistcoat	/'weɪs(t)ˌkəʊt/

Module 6, Lesson 21

body language	/'bɒdi ˌlæŋgwɪdʒ/
compliment	/'kɒmplɪmənt/
confident	/'kɒnfɪd(ə)nt/
controversial	/ˌkɒntrə'vɜ:(r)ʃ(ə)l/
first impression	/ˌfɜ:(r)st ɪm'preʃ(ə)n/
form an opinion	/ˌfɔ:(r)m æn ə'pɪnjən/
greet	/gri:t/
introduce	/ˌɪntrə'dju:s/
nervous	/'nɜ:(r)vəs/
stare	/steə(r)/

Module 6, Lesson 22

addicted to	/ə'dɪktɪd ˌtu:/
alarm	/ə'lɑ:(r)m/
anti-social	/ˌænti'səʊʃ(ə)l/
chat	/tʃæt/
emergency situation	/ɪ'mɜ:(r)dʒ(ə)nsi ˌsɪtʃueɪʃ(ə)n/
face to face	/ˌfeɪs tu: 'feɪs/
loud	/laʊd/
ring tone	/'rɪŋ ˌtəʊn/
social life	/'səʊʃ(ə)l ˌlaɪf/
useful	/'ju:sf(ə)l/

Module 6, Lesson 23

accent	/'æks(ə)nt/

Module 6, Lesson 24

bark	/bɑ:(r)k/
communicate	/kə'mju:nɪkeɪt/
domestic	/də'mestɪk/
howl	/haʊl/
identify	/aɪ'dentɪfaɪ/
nomad	/'nəʊmæd/
permanent	/'pɜ:(r)mənənt/
sign language	/'saɪn ˌlæŋgwɪdʒ/
vocal organ	/'vəʊk(ə)l ˌɔ:(r)gən/
wander	/'wɒndə(r)/

Module 6, Extra Special

apprentice	/ə'prentɪs/
cellar	/'selə(r)/
make a decision	/ˌmeɪk ə dɪ'sɪʒ(ə)n/
orphan	/'ɔ:(r)f(ə)n/
shriek	/ʃri:k/
workhouse	/'wɜ:(r)kˌhaʊs/

Macmillan Education
Between Towns Road, Oxford OX4 3PP
A division of Macmillan Publishers Limited
Companies and representatives throughout the world

ISBN 978-0-230-40877-7

Designed by Ben Cracknell Studios
Illustrated by Humberto Blanco (Sylvie Poggio Artists Agency),
Tom Connell (Kingpin Media), Marco Cutrufo (Kingpin
Media), Jim Eldridge (Beehive Illustration), James Hart (Sylvie
Poggio Artists Agency), Gary Joynes (Beehive Illustration),
Laura Martinez (Sylvie Poggio Artists Agency), Mark Preston,
Norbert Sipos (Beehive Illustration), John Stokes (Kingpin
Media), Jo Taylor (Sylvie Poggio Artists Agency)
Original cover design by Designers Collective; background
image by iStock

The authors and publishers would like to thank the following for
permission to reproduce their photographic material:

Advertising Archives/ pp62(bl, r), 88(bl, br); **Alamy**/
Arcticphoto p12(t), Alamy/ artpartner-images.com p22(tr),
Alamy/ Thomas Cockrem p7, Alamy/ Denkou Images p17,
Alamy/ Directphoto.org p79(tr), Alamy/ Fancy p26, Alamy/
foodfolio p79(br), Alamy/ Gallo Images pp37(br), 86(b),
Alamy/ Tim Hill pp59(bl), 67(cr), Alamy/ Imagebroker p79(tl),
Alamy/ Images of Africa Photobank p91(l), Alamy/ Image
Source p52(l), Alamy/ Neil Jefferson p59(tr), Alamy/ Juniors
Bildarchiv p76(tr), Alamy/ B O'Kane p13(cb), Alamy/ LOOK
Die Bildagentur der Fotografen GmbH p29(t), Alamy/ Manor
Photography p67(l), Alamy/ Simon Margetson p79(bl), Alamy/
Metta foto p34(tl), Alamy/ Andrew Paterson p59(br), Alamy/
PhotoAlto p58, Alamy/ Radius Images pp10(l), 15, Alamy/
Andres Rodriguez p18(l), Alamy/ Chris Rout p64(br), Alamy/
Branislav Senic p67(r),
Alamy/ tbkmedia.de p76(bl), Alamy/ Penny Tweedie p8(bl),
Alamy/ Rawdon Wyatt p77(bcl); **Corbis**/ AlaskaStock p90(bl),
Corbis/ Peter Andrews p22(bl), Corbis/ Bettmann pp10(r),
32(cl, cr), Corbis/ Camerique/ Classic Stock p32(1950s family),
Corbis/ Chris Cheadle/ All Canada Photos p20, Corbis/ Gerald
& Buff Corsi/ Visuals Unlimited p36(l), 41(tc), Corbis/ Randy
Faris p39(br), Corbis/ Gallo Images p8(br), Corbis/ Rick Gomez
p25(tr), Corbis/ Tim Graham p32(tl), Corbis/ Gavin Hellier/
JAI p43, Corbis/ JGI/ Jamie Grill/ Blend Images p40, Corbis/
Frans Lanting p37(tl), Corbis/ Frank Lukasseck p91(c), Corbis/
Colin McPherson p16, Corbis/ Sol Neelman p25(bl), Corbis/
Christine Reilly p64(bl), Corbis/ Specialist Stock p90(g), Corbis/
Wang Song/ Xinhua Press p25(br), Corbis/ UV Images/ Amana
Images p39(tr), Corbis/ Stuart Westmorland pp46, 90(e, f),
Corbis/ Winfried Wisniewski p91(r), Corbis/ Tim Zurowski/
All Canada Photos p90(tr); **Creatas**/ p32(tr); **Digital Stock**/
p81; **Digital Vision**/ pp37(tr), 41(tl), 89; **Fotolibra**/ Gary
Lucken p77(bl); **Getty**/ pp22(tl, ct, cr, bc), 50(t), 67(cl), 84,
88(t), 90(br), Getty/ Amana Productions Inc p18(c), Getty/
John Guistina p86(t), Getty/ Doug Hamilton p39(tl), Getty/
Gavin Hellier/ JAI p43, Getty/ Jupiter Images p72, Getty/ Ian
Murray p13(t), Getty/ Photodisc p8(tr), Getty/ Susanna Price
p77(br), Getty/ Alan Shapiro pp36(r), 41(tr), Getty/ Ian Spanier
p38(b); **Macmillan Publishers Ltd**/ Haddon Davies p77(tr),
Macmillan Publishers Ltd/ David Tolley p52(r); **Monaco Earth
Day Swim 2008**/ p34(tr); **Nature Picture Library**/ Francis
Abbott p90(d), Nature Picture Library/ Jane Burton p90(tl),
Nature Picture Library/ Steven Kazlowski pp36(c), 41(br);
Photodisc/ p29(c); **Photolibrary**/ Jim Cummins p25(bc),
Photolibrary/ Laura Doss p62(tl), Photolibrary/ Fancy p66,
Photolibrary/ Foodfolio p59(tl), Photolibrary/ Goodshoot
p8(tl), Photolibrary/ Nicole Hill p9, Photolibrary/ Hillcreek
Pictures BV p64(tl), Photolibrary/ Image100 p23, Photolibrary/
Juice Images p13(br), Photolibrary/ Juniors Bildarchiv p37(bl),
Photolibrary/ Lucenet Patrice p77(tl), Photolibrary/ PhotoAlto/
Sandro Di Carlo Darsa p34(br), Photolibrary/ Pixtal Images
p32(bl), Photolibrary/ Superstock Inc p77(c),
Photolibrary/ Harold Taylor p90(ct), Photolibrary/ Yoshio Tomli
Photo Studio p50; **Rex Features**/ 20th Century Fox/ Everett p69,
Rex Features/ Columbia/ Everett p55, Rex Features/ Richard
Crampton p47(l), Rex Features/ Everett Collection p32(vintage
computer), Rex Features/ Eye Ubiquitous p13(bl), Rex Features/
OJO Images p64(tr),
Rex Features/ Sipa Press p22(br), Rex Features/ Warner Bros/
Everett p29(b); **Tom Rielly**/ **Moving Windmills Project** p82;
Still Pictures/ McPhoto/ Blickwinkel p76(br); **Superstock**/ age
fotostock p32(br); **Katie Walter**/ Mike Thornewill p12(b).

Commissioned photography by Lisa Payne: pp 6, 14(l,c,r), 33,
35, 47(r), 60, 73, 74, 75, 78.
Thanks to: Akshay, Conor, Jamie, Jesse, Megan, Suhani.

The authors and publishers would also like to thank Mateja
Janše, Anna Petrenkova, Clare Nielsen-Marsh (freelance editor),
Zoë Spilberg (picture research) and Victoria Townsley-Gaunt
(photography coordinator).

The authors and publishers would like to thank the following for
permission to reproduce the following copyright material:

Material from article 'Why exercise is cool', copyright © 1995–
2010, The Nemours Foundation/Kids Health®, reprinted with
permission; Material from 'Teenager Katie Walter is youngest
person to reach the South Pole' by Chris Smyth, copyright ©
Times Newspapers Limited 2010, first published on Times
Online 08.01.2010, reprinted by permission of the publisher;
Poem and Original recording 'Not Yet My Mother' from The
Blue Book by poet Owen Sheers. Poem copyright © Seren 2000,
Original recording copyright © the Poetry Archive, both used
with permission. Music and lyrics for It's a beautiful day, Shine
and Keep on kindly provided with consent by Pump Audio/
Getty.

Printed and bound in Thailand

2015 2014 2013 2012 2011
10 9 8 7 6 5 4 3 2 1